KU-520-521

ROSES

DAVID SQUIRE

ROSES

DAVID SQUIRE

Illustrated by Vana Haggerty

TIGER BOOKS INTERNATIONAL
LONDON

Designed and conceived by

THE BRIDGEWATER BOOK COMPANY LTD

Art Directed by PETER BRIDGEWATER

Designed by TERRY JEAVONS

Illustrated by VANA HAGGERTY FLS

Edited by MARTYN OLIVER

Managing Editor ANNA CLARKSON

CLB 3506

This edition published in 1995 by

TIGER BOOKS INTERNATIONAL PLC, London

Printed and bound in Singapore

ISBN 1-85501-487-4

CONTENTS

HISTORY OF ROSES

Few flowers are so highly prized as the rose. It is a flower steeped in history and finely woven within the fabric of Man's development. At one stage roses were prized for both their medicinal value and beauty.

Roses belong to the genus Rosa and are mainly native to the cooler parts of the Northern Hemisphere, in Asia (especially China), Europe (including Britain) and North America.

Botanists suggest that there are approaching three thousand species of roses, but the number of good ones is probably no more than one hundred and fifty. And of these, relatively few have contributed to the vast range of garden varieties grown today.

ROSES *featured in many early herbals. In 1597 the barber-surgeon and herbalist John Gerard published his Herball.*

THIS *engraving of knights and ladies in a rose garden appeared in* Das Heldenbuch *(The Book of Heroes) printed in 1477, although known in manuscript form several years earlier. It is a collection of medieval German epics, some from the thirteenth century.*

SPECIES ROSES

The earliest cultivated roses were 'wild' species and the results of their natural and impromptu matings. Examples of species roses are the Dog Rose *(Rosa canina)* and the well-known Sweetbriar or Eglantine *(R. rubiginosa* but earlier called *R. eglanteria).* The natural crossing of the Dog Rose with the French or Provins Rose *(R. gallica)* produced the White Rose of York *(R.* x *alba).*

OLD ROSES

Closely associated with Species Roses are the so-called Old Roses (often known as Old Fashioned Roses). These are varieties that arose as sports or hybrids between Species Roses. Sports are mutations that occur naturally on plants: flowers often reveal a different colour or formation. These Old Roses are usually grouped according to their parentage and were the main ones grown before the introduction of Hybrid Teas.

VICTORIAN MAGIC

During the late Victorian era, novelty and magical tricks were popular, as reported in 1891 by the magazine Scientific Mysteries. *Changing white roses into red ones was achieved – usually to the amazement of a crowd – by sprinkling the petals with aniline crystals and then spraying them with eau-de-Cologne. The petals rapidly become a rich crimson-blush.*

CHINESE ROSES

Until the arrival in Europe of Chinese roses, between 1792 and 1824, the only cultivated roses were Species and Old Roses. The four Chinese roses that were introduced over a span of thirty-two years were hybrids and the result of rose breeding in China for many centuries. They introduced colours previously unknown in European roses. Many new types were created, such as Hybrid China Roses, Hybrid Perpetuals, Noisettes, Boursaults, Bourbon and Tea Roses. Many of these are still popular, and available from specialist nurseries.

The crossing of Hybrid Perpetuals and Tea Roses created the first Hybrid Tea rose in 1867, while, during the early 1920s, Floribundas were produced by the Danish rose breeder Svend Poulsen. Hybrid Tea (Large-flowered Bush Roses) and Floribundas (Cluster-flowered Bush Roses) have proved to be the most popular of all garden roses.

THIS *illustration from* Das Heldenbuch *shows two knights receiving chaplets of roses – together with kisses – from their ladies before going into battle. Other woodcuts from the book are less romantic and reveal the brutality of battle. The book depicts the activites of Dietrich of Bern and the brothers Ortnit and Wolfdietrich, who feature widely in many Germanic legends.*

TYPES OF ROSES

Roses are remarkable deciduous shrubs, and their success owes much to their hardiness and willingness to be domesticated. They pollinate freely between themselves and are also amenable to botanists tampering with their sex-life to create further hybrids and varieties. Additionally, gardeners are easily able to increase their plants by budding or, for some types, by taking cuttings or layering shoots. Indeed, by budding (uniting a desired variety with the root-stock of a variety of known vigour) the creation of plants with a predictable size is enabled. Some root-stocks make it possible to grow roses on ground which otherwise might not be fully satisfactory for them.

These practical qualities have combined to enable nurserymen to widen the colour spectrum, to encourage longer flowering seasons and to tailor a shrub's shape, so as to form bushes, to create standards of several different heights, and to produce beautiful weeping standards.

GRANDIFLORA

This is a term that frequently appears in rose catalogues and books. It is a North American term, and refers to vigorous Floribunda-type varieties of rose with large, shapely, Hybrid Tea-type flowers. 'Queen Elizabeth', introduced in 1954, is an excellent example of the Grandiflora type.

Roses are resilient shrubs, perhaps resenting neglect but nevertheless usually surviving it. However, when correctly planted and established, pruned and fed you will have a shrub with a life expectancy of fifteen or more years. The skills needed to grow roses successfully are detailed on pages 10 to 19.

HYBRID TEA *(Large-flowered Bush Roses) types have long flower stems. Their flowers are initially high-pointed and graceful, later reflexed, and are borne singly or in small clusters (pages 20 to 25).*

FLORIBUNDAS *(Cluster-flowered Bush Roses) bear flowers in large clusters (trusses) and create masses of colour over a long period. They are superb in beds and borders in gardens (pages 26 to 31).*

MINIATURE ROSES *are increasingly popular. They have a diminutive nature, with scaled-down buds, flowers, petals, stems and leaves. Few miniature roses grow more than 38cm/15in high (page 32).*

SPECIES ROSES *are those that at one time could be found growing wild. They include* R. rubrifolia *(now* R. glauca) *which is native to Central and Southern Europe (pages 34 and 35).*

OLD ROSES *include a wide range of old-fashioned types derived through hybridization or as sports from species types. The Bourbon 'La Reine Victoria' is a superb Old Rose (pages 36 to 41).*

MODERN SHRUB ROSES *are later introductions than the Old Roses, but still hybrids between Species and Old Roses. 'Frühlingsgold' is one of these attractive roses (pages 42 and 43).*

SHAPE AND COLOUR

The size of flowers varies widely: some species have eight or less petals, while many Hybrid Tea and Floribunda types have forty or more in each flower. Colours range through most shades, from the brightest white to darkest red, but not a proper blue. This is because the rose family does not have the genetic ability to create blue in the same way as many other plants.

Bush-shaped plants are popular and range from miniatures at only 23cm/9in high to Floribundas 1.8m/6ft or more tall. Some Species and Old Roses have a bush shape, while others are prostrate and ideal for forming ground cover. There are even roses that can be planted in hanging baskets. Climbers and ramblers drench walls, arbours, arches and pergolas in colour, while some clamber into trees.

PATIO ROSES *are a relatively new group and, correctly, are low-growing Floribundas. Most grow between 45cm/1½in and 60cm/2ft high; they have a more robust nature than the miniatures (page 33).*

CLIMBERS *have larger flowers than ramblers and more permanent growth. Also, they have the ability to repeat-flower after their first flowering. 'Golden Showers' is a well-known climber (pages 44 and 45).*

RAMBLERS *are a group with varied origins. They have supple stems which develop mainly from the plant's base. 'Albertine' is ideal for growing over pergolas, arches and arbours (pages 46 and 47).*

SOIL AND SITE

Unless the soil and site create the right environment for roses, long-term success is in doubt. All soils have their advantages and disadvantages: clay soils are sticky and heavy, slow to warm up in spring and likely to be badly drained. But they are usually rich in nutrients and retain them for longer than well-drained types. Sandy soils are light, well-drained and easily worked. They warm up quickly in spring but are usually devoid of plant foods, which regularly need to be replenished.

OPTIMUM SOIL

This should be neither too heavy nor light and sandy. Heavy soil can be improved by the installation of drains, double digging and the incorporation of decomposed compost or manure. The addition of sharp sand encourages better drainage, but is expensive over a large area. Sandy soil is also improved by adding compost or manure, but this decomposes rapidly in well-aerated soil and has to be replenished regularly in the form of a mulch.

1. SINGLE DIGGING *is when soil is dug to the depth of a spade's blade. First, dig a trench, 25cm/10in deep and 38cm/15in wide.*

2. PLACE *decomposed compost or manure in the trench. Use a spade to invert pieces of soil, 10cm/4in thick, into the trench.*

3. CONTINUE *digging the bed, inverting soil into the trench. At the end, fill the last trench with soil taken from the first one.*

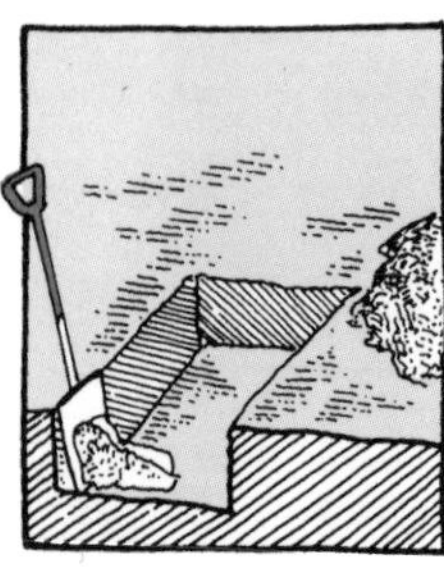

1. DOUBLE DIGGING *is when soil is dug to the depth of two spade blades. Form a trench 25cm/10in deep and 45cm/1½ ft wide.*

2. USE A *garden fork to turn over the soil in the base of the trench, at the same time adding decomposed compost or manure.*

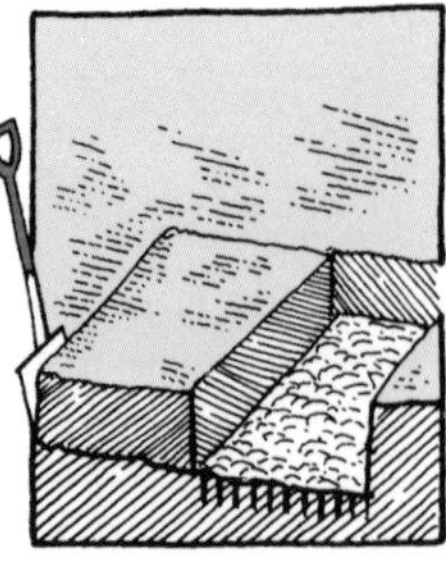

3. THEN, *use a spade to turn over the top spadeful and to place it upside down in the base of the trench. Remove all perennial weeds.*

SELECT *a position for roses that is protected from cold winds. A hedge is best, as it filters wind rather than creating strong turbulence on the lee side.*

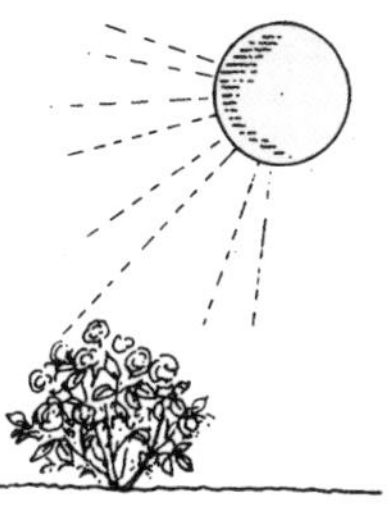

PLENTY *of sun is vital, but a position that offers slight shade in afternoons is also suitable. Sun ripens the wood and helps to produce top-quality flowers.*

FREELY *circulating air around stems and leaves is essential. Do not plant roses under trees or near walls as this will tend to restrict air circulation.*

The nature of soil greatly influences the type of pruning given to roses growing in it. For example, cutting back bush roses encourages the development of strong shoots which later bear flowers. But if the soil is not moist and rich in plant foods, growth is weak (see pages 14 and 15)

Chalky soils can be a problem for roses, which grow best in a pH of 6.0 to 6.5. If the surface soil is too chalky, adding copious amounts of compost or manure helps to reduce alkalinity; the application of acidic nitrogenous fertilizers such as sulphate of ammonia in spring also encourages acidity. However, if the underlying soil is solid chalk, no treatment will reduce the alkalinity. Even digging a hole and filling it with fresh, non-alkaline soil has limited benefit as water in the soil will be chalky and eventually contaminate the area.

The practical solution is to plant roses in raised beds or to select lime-tolerant species such as Albas, Damasks and Hybrid Musks. There are many varieties within these groupings.

CORRECTING ACIDITY

Roses grow best in slightly acid soil, with a pH of 6.0–6.5. Many kits are available to test the soil, so that the amount of lime needed to correct acidity can be assessed. Some kits use chemicals which, when mixed with a soil sample, produce a colour reaction that can be compared with a chart. But for those gardeners who are green–red colour-blind, a probe which indicates the acidity on a dial is much better.

As a guide, the following amounts of lime should decrease the level of acidity by about 1.0 pH.

SOIL	HYDRATED LIME	GROUND LIME-STONE
Clay	610g/sq m (18oz/sq yd)	810g/sq m (24oz/sq yd)
Loam	410g/sq yd (12oz/sq m)	540g/sq m (16oz/sq yd)
Sand	200g/sq m (6oz/sq yd)	270/sq m (8oz/sq yd)

BUYING AND PLANTING

THERE are three main forms in which roses can be bought: 'bare-rooted', 'pre-packed' and 'container-grown'. Each of these forms has both advantages and disadvantages.

• Bare-rooted roses are grown in the open ground in nurseries and dug up during their dormant period (late autumn to late winter) and either sold direct to customers or through mail-order. They usually arrive packed in large, multi-layer paper sacks which have been stitched closed. In earlier times they were wrapped in pyramidal straw bundles. Remove the wrapping and, if your soil is not frozen or waterlogged, plant them immediately. If planting cannot take place directly, but will happen within a week, leave the plants in their packages and place in a cool shed or garage. Where planting cannot be performed within a number of weeks, unpack the plants and bury their roots (known as heeling-in) in a sheltered, well-drained part of a garden.

• Pre-packed roses are grown in the same way as bare-rooted types and dug up during their dormant period. Their roots are then covered with moist peat and the entire plant wrapped in polythene. Unfortunately, this encourages premature growth if kept too warm. These are frequently sold through high street shops. As soon as you get them home, untie the packages and treat in the same way as bare-rooted types.

• Container-grown roses, as the name suggests, have been grown in containers from when they were small plants. Sold throughout the year, they can be planted whenever the soil is neither frozen nor waterlogged. Before planting, check the compost is evenly moist.

WHEN *planting a bare-rooted bush rose, dig a hole 50–60cm/20–24in wide and 20–25cm/8–10in deep. Fork the base and add moist peat. Form a slight mound and spread roots over it. Use a straight stick to check that the union between the variety and roots (just below the lowest stem) is 2.5cm/1in below the surface.*

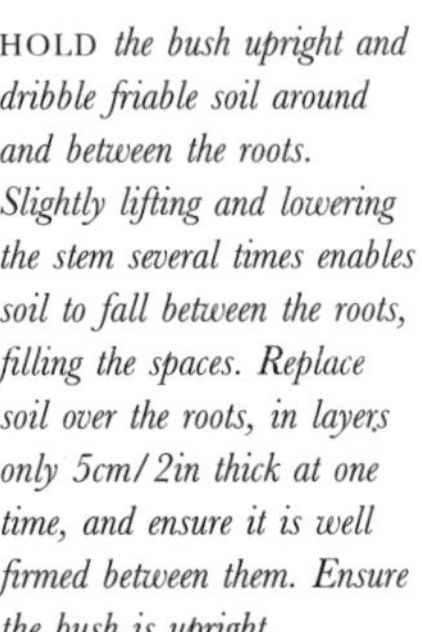

HOLD *the bush upright and dribble friable soil around and between the roots. Slightly lifting and lowering the stem several times enables soil to fall between the roots, filling the spaces. Replace soil over the roots, in layers only 5cm/2in thick at one time, and ensure it is well firmed between them. Ensure the bush is upright.*

CONTINUE *to firm soil in layers around and over the roots until the surface is level. Use the heel of a shoe to ensure it is firm and then use a fork or rake to level the surface. If foot marks are left, water will rest in them. Never fill the hole and cover the roots in one operation, as pockets of air may then be trapped around the roots.*

PREPARING FOR PLANTING

Bare-rooted and pre-packaged roses need to be checked over before they are planted. Cut back damaged shoots to sound wood. Also, prune off shoots with leaves or heps (fruits) on them, as well as thin and twiggy growths. Cut off dead, damaged and excessively long roots, so that they are not more than 30cm/12in long.

To ensure that the roots and stems are plump and full of moisture, immerse them in water for at least twenty-four hours (right).

TRANSPLANTING ESTABLISHED ROSES

If you move to an established garden it is possible a bush rose may need to be moved. If old and neglected, it is best dug up and a new one put in. If young, transplanting is possible during its dormant period, from late autumn to late winter. Replant it in the way recommended for bush roses.

ENSURING ROOTS ARE MOIST

Never plant bare-rooted roses when their roots are dry. Place them in a large bucket deeply filled with clean water for at least twenty-four hours. This ensures that they are plump and full of moisture when planted and able to establish themselves quickly.

If the weather is dry and roses are planted with shrivelled roots, they may die. But if roots are plump and moist they will have a better chance of survival.

PLANTING *container-grown roses needs the same soil preparation as bare-rooted types. Form a hole, place moist peat in the base and position the plant, still in its container. Its top should be 12mm/½in below the surface. Carefully remove the container and pack and firm good soil around it. Water the soil thoroughly.*

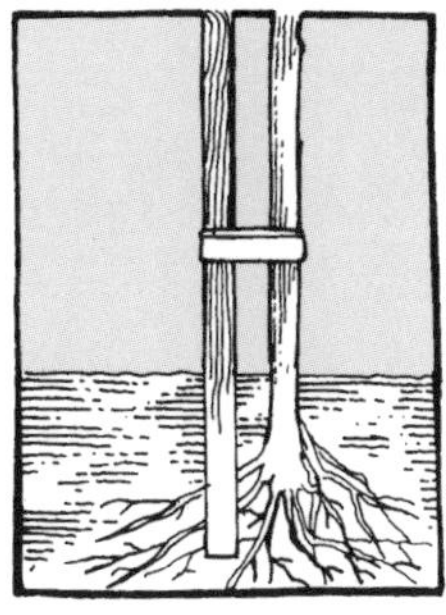

WHEN *planting a standard rose, dig a hole, form a mound and place moist peat over it. Insert a stake on the windward side, about 7.5cm/3in off-centre. Position the plant and check it is slightly deeper than before. Spread out the roots and firm soil over them. Tie the stem firmly to the stake in three places.*

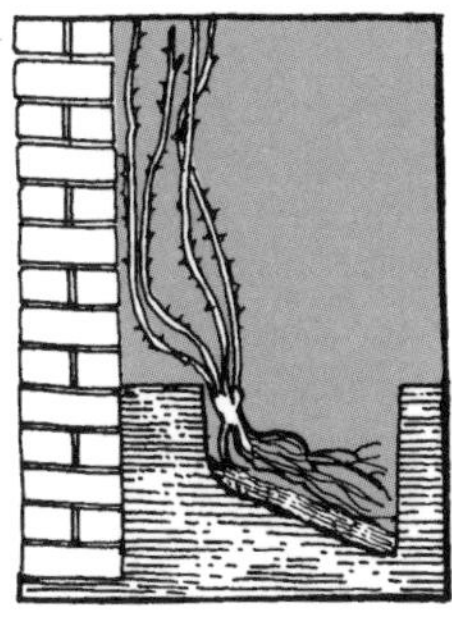

TO PLANT *a climber against a wall, position the roots not less than 38cm/15in from it. Dig a hole and fill it with moist peat. Position the roots in the hole and check that they are slightly deeper than before. Spread and firm good soil over and between the roots. Thoroughly water the soil several times.*

PRUNING

PRUNING is a yearly job and one that must not be neglected, especially with Hybrid Tea and Floribunda types. These are roses that flower on shoots produced earlier in the same year.

Every rose expert has a particular opinion about the best time to prune roses, but the consensus is:

- Established bushes, together with autumn and winter-planted ones, are best pruned in early spring, just as growth begins but before leaves start to appear.
- Bushes planted in spring should be pruned immediately after they have been planted.
- To prevent bushes being rocked by strong winter winds and their roots loosened, cut back long stems in early winter. Then, in spring they can be pruned properly. Always pick up and burn shoots which have been cut off.

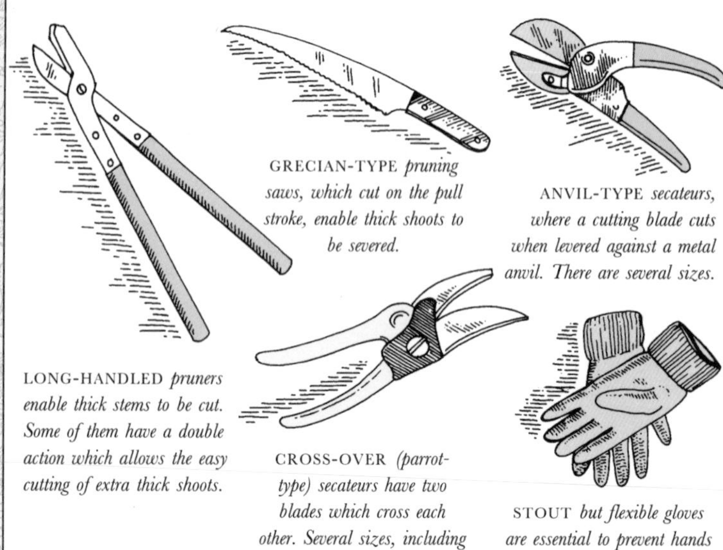

GRECIAN-TYPE *pruning saws, which cut on the pull stroke, enable thick shoots to be severed.*

ANVIL-TYPE *secateurs, where a cutting blade cuts when levered against a metal anvil. There are several sizes.*

LONG-HANDLED *pruners enable thick stems to be cut. Some of them have a double action which allows the easy cutting of extra thick shoots.*

CROSS-OVER *(parrot-type) secateurs have two blades which cross each other. Several sizes, including left-handed types.*

STOUT *but flexible gloves are essential to prevent hands being ripped by thorns.*

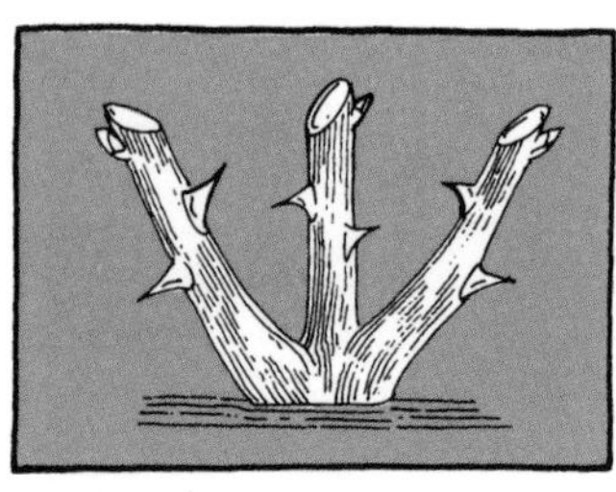

MAKING *the correct type of pruning cut is essential. Ragged and badly-positioned cuts encourage stems to decay. Also, such cuts are unsightly. A slightly sloping cut (shown above) is correct: about 6mm/¼in above a strong, healthy, outward-facing bud.*

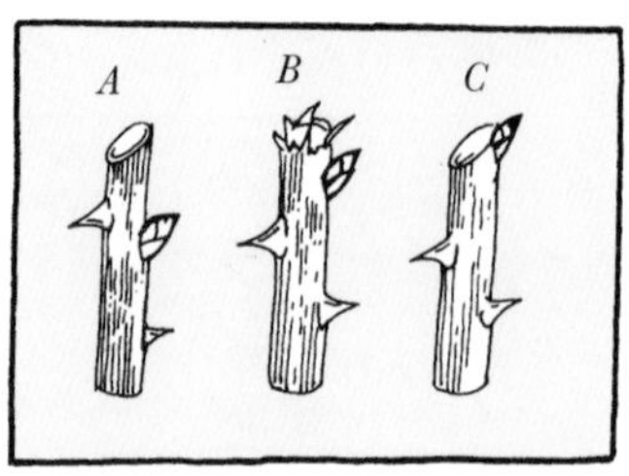

THE ABOVE *illustration shows the types of cut not to make: (A) is too far above the bud, encouraging it to die back; (B) is the result of using blunt or insufficiently large secateurs; (C) is too close to the bud, which eventually may become insecure and topple over.*

PRUNING BUSH ROSES

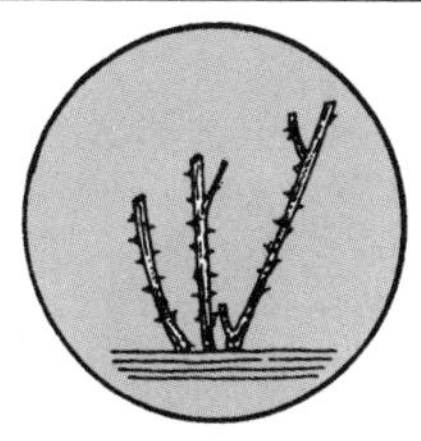

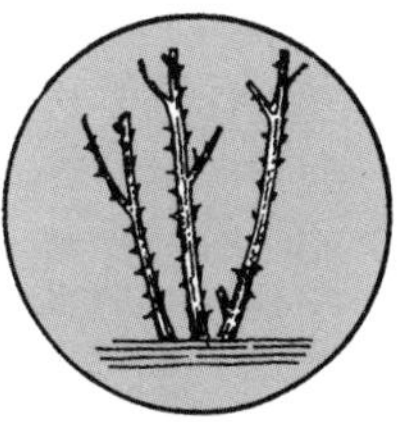

1. HARD PRUNING *(or Low Pruning). Stems of bush (Hybrid Tea and Floribunda) roses are cut back to within three or four buds of the plant's base, leaving stems 13–15cm/ 5–6in long. This method is only suitable for use on newly-planted bush roses and weak-growing Hybrid Teas.*

2. MODERATE PRUNING *(also known as Medium Pruning) involves cutting back stems by about a half of their length. Weaker shoots, however, must be pruned back hard. This method of pruning is ideal for most Hybrid Teas and Floribundas and is the system adopted by most rose growers.*

3. LIGHT PRUNING *(also known as Long Pruning) involves cutting off the top third of all shoots. Ensure the cuts are made just above an outward-facing bud. This system is used to limit the growth of very vigorous Hybrid Tea roses as it does not subsequently encourage the development of further strong shoots.*

INITIAL STAGES IN PRUNING When pruning bush roses – and before deciding to 'hard', 'moderate' or 'light' prune them (see above) – the first step is to remove damaged and diseased shoots. Cut them back to below the damaged area, to sound wood. Then, cut out thin and weak shoots, as well as those that cross the bush's centre and cause congestion. If these are left, the amount of light and air reaching shoots is diminished. Cut out shoots that rub against each other, as this encourages the entry of diseases and may cause shoots to die back.

Cut out unripe stems which, if left, could be damaged by severe winter weather. A test for the maturity of shoots is to snap off several thorns. It they break easily, the wood is mature; but if they tear or bend, it indicates immaturity.

PRUNING STANDARD ROSES

As soon as standard roses are received during their dormant period, plant them and cut back strong stems to a point 15cm/ 6in from the union (where they were budded at the top of the stem). This reduces the area of foliage exposed to the buffeting of the wind.

During the following year, shoots develop which will bear flowers in summer. In mid-autumn or early winter, cut off the tips of stems. Completely cut out soft and immature shoots.

In late winter of the following year, cut out to their bases all dead, crossing or weak shoots. Also, remove dead and twiggy shoots. At the same time, prune back all shoots that developed during the previous year to 15cm/ 6in from their base, and lateral shoots to about 10cm/ 4in of their point or origin. Hybrid Tea standard roses are pruned more severely than Floribunda varieties.

LOOKING AFTER ROSES

PART of the pleasure of roses is looking after them. Regular attention is essential, from spring to autumn as well as protecting them during winter, especially when they are growing in cold and exposed positions.

Feeding (page 18) and pruning (pages 14 and 15) are important, and here are some other jobs that need attention. If bush roses such as Hybrid Teas and Floribundas are neglected their life-span is dramatically reduced.

DURING *summer, remove sucker shoots growing from below soil level. Remove some soil and trace the sucker to its base. Wear a stout glove and pull off the sucker, close to its base. Replace and firm soil around the root: loose soil encourages suckers.*

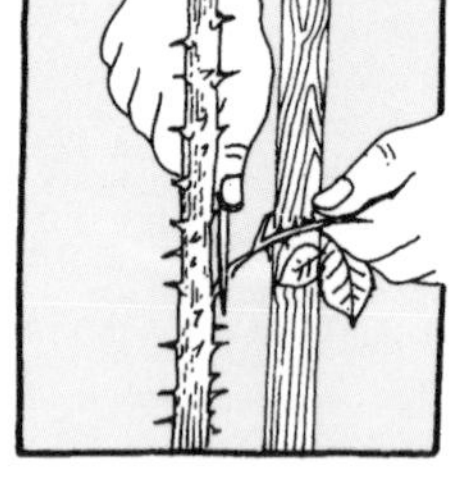

SUCKERS *sometimes grow from the stem of a standard rose. Do not pull them off (in the same way as those at ground level). Instead, use a sharp knife to cut the sucker flush with the stem. Avoid unnecessary cutting, as this may damage the stem.*

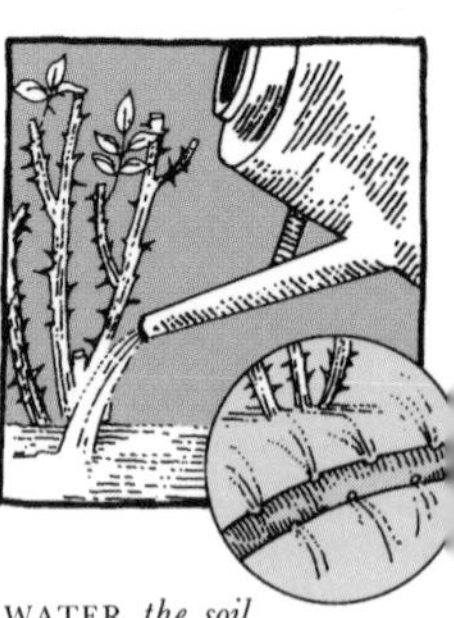

WATER *the soil around roses regularly in summer, especially during droughts. Thoroughly soak the soil; just dampening the surface does more harm than good. Perforated hose laid on the soil makes this job easier and spreads water evenly.*

FROM *spring to autumn, remove weeds by shallow hoeing. This also breaks up crusty surface soil and enables air and moisture to penetrate. But hoeing too deeply damages roots and encourages suckers.*

REMOVE *dead flowers from bush roses. Cut the stem back to slightly above the second or third leaf below the dead flowers, removing the complete truss. Do not dead-head Shrub Roses grown for their heps (fruits).*

APPLY *chemical weed-killers through a dribble-bar attached to a watering-can solely used for that purpose. Only apply weed-killers when the weather is dry and there is little or no wind to disturb the spray.*

The mulch should not touch the stem.

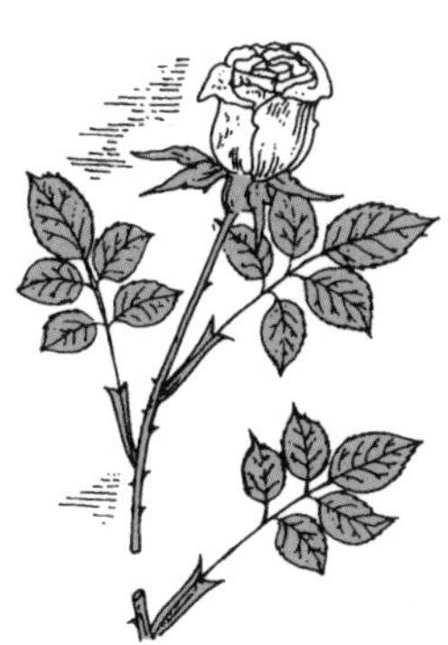

LARGE *Hybrid Tea flowers (often for exhibiting) can be produced by disbudding the blooms. As soon as the small buds growing from the leaf-joints just below the main flower are large enough to handle, bend them sideways so that they snap off cleanly. Make sure you do not tear the stem.*

MULCH *roses to prevent the growth of weeds, conserve soil moisture, keep it cool and provide some nutrients. In spring, shallowly hoe the soil, remove any weeds, apply a feed and water the soil. Then, apply a 10cm/4in-thick layer of well-decayed garden compost or manure over the soil.*

WHEN *cutting fresh roses for home decoration, use sharp scissors or a knife. Cut stems just above a leaf-joint and do not take too many from one plant, or from the same position. Preferably, cut the stems early in the morning, when they are full of moisture. Place them in deep, cool water.*

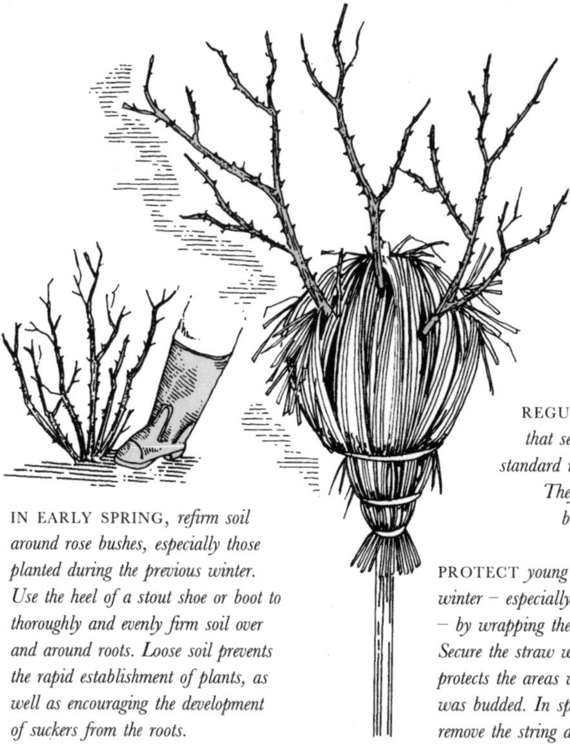

REGULARLY *check ties that secure the stem of a standard rose to its support. They should be secure but not constrictive.*

IN EARLY SPRING, *refirm soil around rose bushes, especially those planted during the previous winter. Use the heel of a stout shoe or boot to thoroughly and evenly firm soil over and around roots. Loose soil prevents the rapid establishment of plants, as well as encouraging the development of suckers from the roots.*

PROTECT *young standard roses in winter – especially in exposed areas – by wrapping the head in straw. Secure the straw with string. This protects the areas where the plant was budded. In spring, carefully remove the string and straw.*

FEEDING

BUSH roses must be regularly fed to encourage the yearly development of fresh shoots that later bear flowers. Feed them three times a year, once in spring, then in early summer and, lastly, in mid-summer. Do not feed them after this time as soft shoots will be produced that will be damaged by winter frosts. Always combine the application of a mulch with the feeding programme; first hoe shallowly and remove weeds, apply the fertilizer and water in (if granular or powder). Only then should a mulch be applied. Once a mulch is in position, use a proprietary liquid feed at the recommended strength – never experiment.

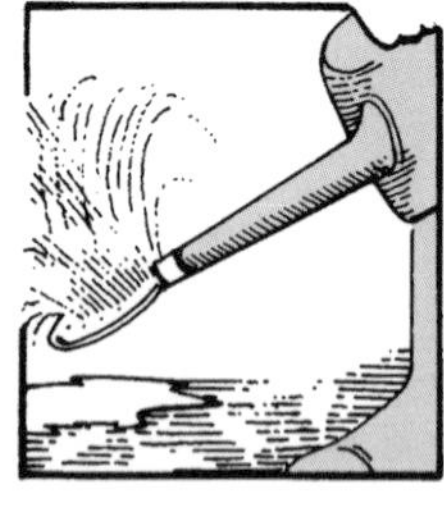

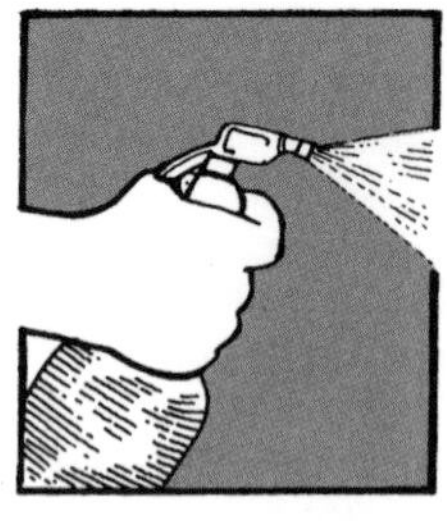

DUSTING *the soil around roses with a granular or powder fertilizer in spring and summer is the traditional way to feed them. Shallowly hoe the fertilizer into the surface, then lightly but thoroughly water the soil.*

APPLYING *a liquid rose fertilizer diluted in water around plants provides readily-available food for roses. Make several applications, during spring and summer. Always keep to the recommended strength.*

FOLIAR *feeding is relatively new and provides an 'instant' tonic for plants as it rapidly gets into a plant's sap-stream. It is an ideal method of feeding for improving exhibition plants at the very last moment.*

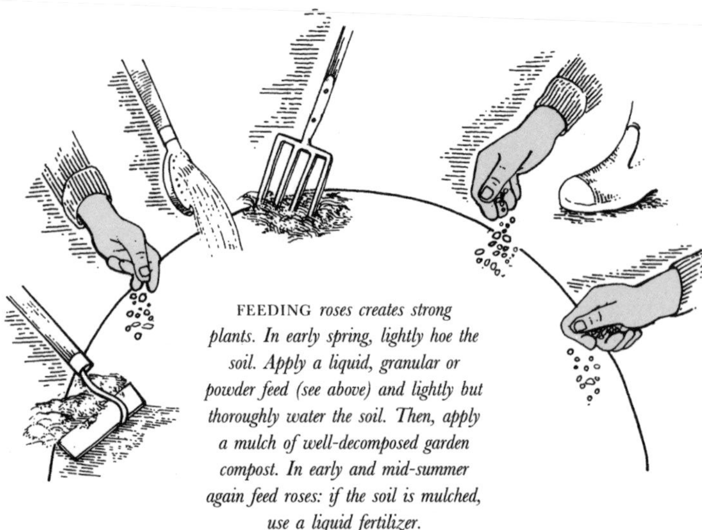

FEEDING *roses creates strong plants. In early spring, lightly hoe the soil. Apply a liquid, granular or powder feed (see above) and lightly but thoroughly water the soil. Then, apply a mulch of well-decomposed garden compost. In early and mid-summer again feed roses: if the soil is mulched, use a liquid fertilizer.*

EXHIBITION ROSES

WHEN growing roses becomes a passionate hobby, exhibiting a few blooms is a logical trend. The season before exhibiting your own roses, inspect those displayed by experts. There is much to learn and listening to the judges more than pays off when exhibiting your own. Carefully read the rules of the show and do not be tempted to enter too many blooms during the first season of exhibiting your own roses.

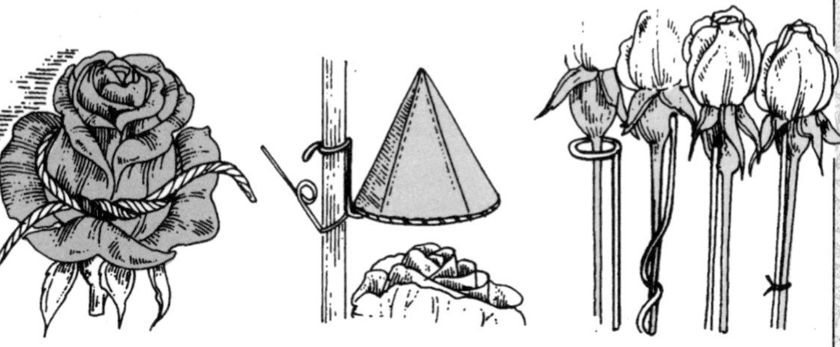

TYING *soft, thick, white wool around a half-open, dry bloom two or three days before the show helps to lengthen the petals and to create an attractive outline. Each morning, slightly loosen and re-secure the tie.*

A CONICAL *bloom-protector secured to a stake about two weeks before the show helps to give protection during a wet season. Water spotting is then prevented. Ensure the cone does not drip rain water on other blooms.*

WIRING *roses with weak necks gives them support (but check that the rules allow this). There are two methods: either encircle the stem with a loop or coiled wire, or pierce the bud with a wire, then tie it to the stem.*

DISPLAYING EXHIBITION ROSES

TRADITIONALLY, *roses were displayed in specimen boxes, holding six or twelve blooms. Fresh green moss was packed in the box and glass tubes positioned so that when the blooms were added they did not touch. Graduate the flower sizes.*

DISPLAYS *in bowls are very attractive. Avoid colour clashes where mixed varieties are displayed; position pastel shades between those with strong colours and form an even outline. Ensure that the bowl's size, colour and shape are suitable.*

VASES HOLDING *three or six blooms are popular in some shows. The vases are usually provided: pack with short rushes and remove lower thorns and leaves from the stems. Ensure the blooms do not touch. Fill the vase with clean water.*

HYBRID TEAS
White, Ivory and Cream

 HYBRID Tea roses are often considered to be the aristocrats of the rose world. They have long stems and flowers, initially with a high-pointed and graceful outline. Later they open and the petals bend backwards.

In some books, Hybrid Tea roses are referred to by their new name, Large-flowered Bush Roses (sometimes shortened to LF Bush), but mostly they are still known as Hybrid Teas or HTs.

Their colour range is wide and from here until page 25 they are grouped according to their shade, from white to blends of orange.

WHITE HYBRID TEAS

These are not dramatic. Instead, they introduce a cool, restful aura to both gardens and flower arrangements indoors. There are many excellent varieties to choose from, including:

• 'Elizabeth Harkness': Scented, ivory flowers with a touch of pink and gold. Bushes grow about 82cm/32in high and 60cm/2ft wide. It is free-flowering and equally good in beds or for cutting to decorate rooms indoors.

• 'Evening Star': Large, lightly-scented, white flowers borne singly or in clusters on bushes about 90cm/3ft high and 60cm/2ft wide. Attractive leaves. Each flower has about twenty-five petals.

• 'Message': Large, lightly-scented white blooms with a greenish cast. Growth is upright, about 90cm/3ft high and spreading to 60cm/2ft.

• 'Pascali': Long-lasting, large, white blooms which are resistant to damage from rain. Growth is upright, about 75cm/2½ft high and about 50cm/20in wide.

• 'Peaudouce': Also known as 'Elina', it has moderately-scented, ivory flowers with a lemon centre. Bushes grow 1m/2½ft high and about 75cm/2½ft wide.

• 'Polar Star': Large, white flowers borne on strong, upright stems. Bushes grow about 1m/3½ft high and 72cm/28in wide. An ideal white variety for cutting.

• 'Silver Wedding': Lightly-scented, creamy white blooms borne on bushy plants about 50cm/20in high and wide.

'POLAR STAR' *has white flowers and richly dark-green foliage.*

ROSE HIP JAM

Boil washed rose heps (fruit) in an equal amount of water for 15 minutes. Strain, add sugar and boil until thickened.

HYBRID TEAS
Yellow and Gold

YELLOW Hybrid Teas have a richness which never fails to capture attention and in midsummer it helps to recall the brightness and vitality of spring.

Yellow is a colour that remains visible for a long time in the increasing darkness of evenings, long after red and scarlet have been lost in the twilight. They are therefore superb for planting around or near to the edges of terraces and patios.

YELLOW HYBRID TEAS

Yellow is an all-embracing colour and ranges from light yellow, with flushes of pink, to those totally saturated in yellow. Varieties to choose from include:

- 'Dutch Gold': Strongly-scented, large, golden-yellow blooms which do not fade with age. Bushes are vigorous, growing to about 1m/3½ft high and about 75cm/2½ft wide.
- 'Freedom': Lightly-scented, rich, bright-yellow flowers on bushes with an upright stance, 75cm/2½ft high and 60cm/2ft wide.
- 'Grandpa Dickson': Lightly-scented, pale-yellow blooms which, in hot weather, assume pink flushes. Resistant to rain damage, it grows 75cm/2½ft high and 50cm/20in wide.
- 'Miss Harp': Moderately-scented, deep bronze-yellow flowers that are resistant to damage from wet weather. Bushes are about 82cm/32in high and 60cm/2ft wide.
- 'Peace': Perhaps the best known of all roses, with lightly-scented, large, light yellow flowers flushed pink. Bushes grow 1.2m/4ft high and 90cm/3ft wide.
- 'Peer Gynt': Bright yellow flowers with pink tints on their edges. Bushes have a compact nature, about 82cm/32in high and 60cm/2ft wide.
- 'Simba': Lightly-scented, clear-yellow flowers which appear in flushes. The blooms, which are resistant to weather damage, are borne on bushes 60cm/2ft high and 50cm/20in wide.
- 'Sunblest': Light scent and bright yellow flowers borne prolifically on bushes 90cm/3ft high and 60cm/2ft wide. An excellent variety for cutting to decorate rooms.
- 'Valencia': Moderately-scented, large, light amber-yellow blooms borne on bushes about 90cm/3ft high and 60cm/2ft wide.

'SIMBA' *is clear yellow, with foliage that is resistant to damage from wet weather. Plants are compact and full of leaves.*

HYBRID TEAS
Pink and Blush

PINK and blush covers a wide spectrum of colours, from pinkish-white to light red, and between these is the classic pink with a demure but warm nature. Pink roses – like red ones – have romantic associations and for this reason alone are well worth growing.

There are many varieties to consider and they include:

• 'Abbeyfield Rose': Deep rosy-pink flowers on bushes 60cm/2ft high and wide. It is an ideal variety for growing in small areas.

• 'Admiral Rodney': Large, moderately-scented, pale rose-pink petals with pink reverses. Bushes are moderately vigorous, about 60cm/2ft high and wide.

• 'Blessings': Large, moderately-scented, rosy salmon-pink blooms on vigorous, upright bushes, sometimes 1.2m/4ft high and 75cm/2½ft wide.

'PAUL SHIRVILLE' *has beautiful pink flowers on shrubby plants with shiny, dark foliage.*

• 'Mary Donaldson': Scented, classically high-centred, salmon-pink flowers borne singly or in wide sprays. It is ideal in beds in gardens and grows about 90cm/3ft high and 60cm/2ft wide.

• 'Paul Shirville': Fragrant, large soft salmon-pink flowers that are ideal in gardens and for cutting to decorate homes. Bushes grow 75cm/2½ft high and wide.

• 'Pink Favorite': Popular in North America, with large, deep pink flowers with high centres. Bushes grow to 75cm/2½ft high and 60cm/2ft wide.

• 'Pink Peace': Well-scented, large deep-pink flowers on upright growth. Bushes grow 1m/3½ft high and about 75cm/3ft wide.

• 'Prima Ballerina': Scented, large deep rose-pink flowers – often said to be cherry-pink. Superb in beds in gardens, growing to about 1m/3½ft high and 60cm/2ft wide.

• 'Royal Highness': Well-known in North America, with large classically-shaped, moderately fragrant, pearly-pink flowers on bushes about 1m/3½ft high and 72cm/28in wide.

• 'Savoy Hotel': Lightly-scented large, light pink flowers with deep tones. The bushes are 90cm/3ft high and 60cm/2ft wide.

• 'Silver Jubilee': Lightly-scented large and shapely peach-pink flowers on bushes 1m/3½ft high and 60cm/2ft wide.

• 'Wendy Cussons': Large very fragrant, cherry-red to deep pink flowers on bushes 90cm/3ft high and 60cm/2ft wide.

HYBRID TEAS
Crimson, Scarlet and Vermilion

THESE are dramatic colours and can soon dominate white, yellow and pink varieties if used in large and dominant groups. It is often better to have a complete bed of these colours than to run the risk of overwhelming lighter colours planted nearby.

These colours are so saturated that in twilight they soon appear black, but in bright sunlight they are dominant and eye-catching.

There are many varieties to choose from:

'VELVET FRAGRANCE' *forms a dominant bush, with dark green leaves and a vigorous stance.*

• 'Alexander': Slightly-fragrant, vermilion red flowers, ideal in beds in gardens as well as for cutting and displaying indoors. Bushes grow up to 1.5m/5ft high and 75cm/2½ft wide.

• 'Big Chief': Exceptionally large, deep crimson flowers on vigorous, upright growth. Bushes grow about 1m/3½ft high and about 60cm/2ft wide.

• 'Deep Secret': Fragrant, deep crimson flowers. It is said to be the darkest of all red roses. Bushes are vigorous, up to 90cm/3ft high and 75cm/2½ft wide.

• 'Ernest H. Morse': Fragrant, large, crimson flowers borne prolifically through summer. It is ideal in flower beds and for cutting to decorate homes. Bushes grow about 75cm/2½ft high and 60cm/2ft wide.

• 'Fragrant Cloud': Popular variety, with fragrant, dusky-scarlet flowers on vigorous bushes about 75cm/2½ft high and 60cm/2ft wide.

• 'Papa Meilland': Large, blackish-crimson and velvet-like flowers on plants growing to 90cm/3ft high and 60cm/2ft wide.

• 'Red Devil': Large, exhibition-type, fragrant blooms on bushes which grow to about 1m/3½ft high and 75cm/2½ft wide.

• 'Royal William': Fragrant, deep red blooms on vigorous bushes which reach 1m/3½ft high and 75cm/2½ft wide.

• 'Ruby Wedding': Slightly-fragrant, ruby-crimson flowers borne on branching bushes, about 75cm/2½ft high and 60cm/2ft wide.

• 'Super Star': Moderately-scented, large, vermilion flowers on bushes about 90cm/3ft high and 75cm/2½ft wide.

• 'Velvet Fragrance': Large, fragrant, dark velvet-crimson flowers on bushes 1m/3½ft high and 72cm/28in wide.

HYBRID TEAS
Apricot, Orange and Copper

THESE are warm colours; they do not have the brightness and vitality of yellow, neither do they have the fiery nature of red. Instead, they have a near undefinable quality that has led to some varieties being classified variously as orange or soft red. For example, 'Cheshire Life' is usually put among the oranges, but occasionally with the reds.

There are many varieties with these colours to choose from, and these include:

• 'Apricot Silk': Lightly-scented, large, orange-red blooms with a silky sheen. It is ideal for cutting and displaying indoors, as it has long stems and the blooms last for a long time when cut. Bushes grow about 90cm/3ft high and 60cm/2ft wide.

• 'Beauté': Moderately-scented, large, apricot-orange blooms on vigorous, branching bushes up to 75cm/2½ft high and 60cm/2ft wide.

• 'Bettina': Medium-size, orange blooms with reddish veining. It is ideal in flower arrangements. Bushes grow 75cm/2½ft high and 60cm/2ft wide.

• 'Cheshire Life': Moderately-scented, large blooms usually described as orange, but occasionally orange-red and vermilion-orange. Bushes grow 75cm/2½ft high and 60cm/2ft wide.

• 'Dawn Chorus': Develops masses of slightly-scented, glowing-orange flowers with a yellow base. Bushes grow to 90cm/3ft high and 75cm/2½ft wide.

• 'Diorama': Moderately-scented, large, yellowish-orange flowers flushed red. Bushes are branching and about 75cm/2½ft high and 60cm/2ft wide.

• 'Doris Tysterman': Lightly-scented, orange-red flowers often described as tangerine. Bushes grow up to 1.2m/4ft high and 75cm/2½ft wide.

• 'Fulton Mackay': Moderately-scented, golden apricot blooms on upright growth on bushes 75cm/2½ft high and 60cm/2ft wide.

• 'Johnnie Walker': Large, apricot-coloured blooms on upright and branching bushes, 1m/3½ft high and 75cm/2½ft wide.

• 'Just Joey': Fragrant, large, coppery orange flowers that pale towards their edges. It is ideal in flower beds as well as a cut flower for home decoration. Bushes grow 75cm/2½ft high and 60cm/2ft wide.

'JUST JOEY', *with coppery-orange flowers, is ideal for planting in beds in gardens as well as for cutting to display indoors.*

- 'L'Oreal Trophy': Lightly-scented, large, bright orange-salmon flowers on upright bushes, about 1.2m/4ft high and 75cm/2½ft wide.
- 'Lover's Meeting': Lightly-scented, reddish-orange blooms on vigorous, branching stems. Bushes grow 60cm/2ft high and wide.
- 'Princess Royal': Spicily-scented, golden apricot flowers with a hint of bronze. The blooms have a classical shade, with high centres, and are borne on bushes 82cm/32in high and 60cm/2ft wide.
- 'Remember Me': Fragrant, large, rich coppery orange blooms borne in sprays on bushes 90cm/3ft high and 60cm/2ft wide.
- 'Rosemary Harkness': Sweetly-fragrant, medium-sized, orange-yellow blooms blended with salmon. It is ideal when grown in beds. The bushes have a branching habit, 75cm/2½ft high and about the same in width.
- 'Royal Romance': Classically shaped, with moderately-scented, large, salmon-pink and peach flowers borne amid bushy growth. Bushes grow 75cm/21.2ft high and 60cm/2ft wide. 'Whisky Mac' is one of its parents.
- 'The Lady': Fragrant, large, honey-yellow blooms edged in salmon and borne in wide sprays. Bushes have an upright nature, growing to about 90cm/3ft high and 60cm/ 2ft wide.
- 'Troika': Moderately-scented, large, reddish-orange flowers with yellow and pink flushes. It is ideal for planting in flower beds, as well as for cutting for home decoration – the flowers are shapely, do not fade and have long stems. Bushes grow about 90cm/3ft high and 75cm/2½ft wide.
- 'Whisky Mac': Strongly-scented, large, golden apricot flowers on bushes 75cm/2½ft high and 60cm/2ft wide. The young foliage is reddish and very attractive.

'TROIKA' *has reddish-orange flowers with yellow and pink flushes; it is ideal as a cut flower.*

'BLUE' ROSES

It is probable that no true-blue rose will ever be created, as the blue pigment, delphinidin, is not present in the rose family. Nevertheless, two varieties come quite close to achieving the 'impossible'.

- *'Blue Parfum': Strongly-scented, large, mauve-pink flowers on bushes about 75cm/2½ft high and 60cm/2ft wide.*
- *'Blue Moon': This is considered to be the best 'blue', with lemon-scented, lilac-mauve blooms borne on upright and branching stems. Bushes grow about 90cm/3ft high and 60cm/2ft wide. It is prized by flower arrangers.*

FLORIBUNDAS
White and Cream

FLORIBUNDAS have a more relaxed and informal nature than Hybrid Teas and are superb in beds in gardens, either on their own or mixed with shrubs and other plants. Floribundas are now properly known as Cluster-flowered Bush Roses (sometimes shortened to CF Bush), but invariably in rose catalogues they are still listed as Floribunda (occasionally shortened to Flor).

These floriferous roses flower during the latter part of early summer and into mid-summer, with repeat-flowering later. Their range of colours is wide, and they are described between this page and page 31.

'MARGARET MERRIL' *has large, high-centred, blush-white flowers with a satin sheen. The dark green foliage is resistant to diseases.*

WHITE FLORIBUNDAS

There is a surprisingly small range of white floribundas.

• 'Grace Abounding': Moderately-scented, with showy clusters of creamy, buff-white flowers borne amid shrubby growth up to 90cm/3ft high and 75cm/2½ft wide.

• 'Iceberg': Lightly-scented with large, showy clusters of white flowers borne freely on bushes about 82cm/32in high and 60cm/2ft wide. Unfortunately, during hot weather the flowers become slightly pink. Often it continues to flower into late autumn and occasionally well into winter.

• 'Ivory Fashion': Lightly-fragrant, ivory-white, semi-double and large flowers that open flat. Sometimes, they shade to pale buff in the centre and during wet seasons are susceptible to black spot. Bushes are vigorous, up to 90cm/3ft high and 75cm/2½ft wide.

• 'Margaret Merril': Strongly and richly-scented, large but dainty, high-centred blush-white blooms. They are prized for their satin sheen. Bushes are upright, to about 82cm/32in and about 60cm/2ft wide. The dark green foliage tends to be resistant to damage from disease.

• 'Yvonne Rabier': Although introduced in 1910, before Floribundas were created, it has a similar nature and therefore is included here. It is a cross between *Rosa wichuraiana* and a Polyantha. It bears clusters of fragrant, milky white, small blooms on bushy yet compact plants about 45cm/1½ft high and wide. It only needs light pruning.

This bushy but low-growing rose is listed in some rose catalogues as a Dwarf Polyantha.

FLORIBUNDAS
Yellow and Gold

THESE, like yellow Hybrid Teas, have a dramatic impact on a garden, especially when seen en masse. And because they have more flowers their influence is even more apparent. There are many varieties to choose from, some bold and strong, others demure.

- 'Allgold': Lightly-scented, with large clusters of small, buttercup-yellow flowers on branching bushes 60cm/2ft high and 50cm/20in wide. It is often thought to be one of the best yellow-flowered floribundas.
- 'Amber Queen': Well-scented, amber-yellow flowers borne in large clusters. Bushes grow about 50cm/20in high and 60cm/24in wide. When young, the leaves are reddish, but slowly become dark green. Upright growth.
- 'Arthur Bell': Well-scented, golden yellow flowers borne singly and in clusters on vigorous, upright bushes about 82cm/32in high and 60cm/2ft wide.
- 'Bright Smile': Moderately-scented, bright yellow flowers borne in clusters on plants about 45cm/1½ft high and wide.
- 'Burma Star': Scented, large, light amber flowers borne on upright bushes, about 1.2m/4ft high and 60cm/2ft wide.
- 'Golden Years': Lightly-scented, large, richly golden yellow flowers borne in clusters on bushes 72cm/28in high and 60cm/24in wide. Plenty of foliage.
- 'Honeymoon': Moderately-scented, medium-sized and rosette-shaped canary-yellow flowers on vigorous growth. Growing to about 90cm/3ft high and 60cm/2ft wide, this bush has handsome foliage.

'MOUNTBATTEN'
has large, mimosa-yellow flowers on bushes with a shrub-like stance.

- 'Korresia': Scented, bright yellow flowers with wavy petals. It is superb when planted in flower beds and for cutting to decorate rooms indoors. Bushes grow about 75cm/2½ft high and 60cm/2ft wide.
- 'Mountbatten': Moderately-scented, large, mimosa-yellow flowers borne in small clusters. It is shrub-like and grows 1.2m/4ft high and 82cm/32in wide. A strong, tall and bushy variety.
- 'Princess Alice': Lightly-scented, medium-sized, bright yellow flowers borne in large clusters on bushes 1m/3½ft high and 60cm/2ft high.
- 'Sunsilk': Lightly-scented, large, lemon-yellow flowers borne on upright growth on bushes 82cm/32in high and 60cm/24in wide.

FLORIBUNDAS
Pink and Blush

THESE are reserved and demure colours, neither clinical and pure, like white, nor saturated with colour as are the dominant reds. Indeed, pink is a desaturated red and contains only a small proportion of red pigments. The range of pink varieties varies widely, from those with only a small amount of pink to those only a few shades less than red.

• 'Chanelle': Moderately-scented, creamy pink flowers, although sometimes described as shell-pink and amber-pink. The growth is bushy and plants grow about 75cm/2½ft high and 60cm/2ft wide.

• 'City of Leeds': Slightly-fragrant, medium-sized, blush salmon-pink flowers borne on bushy, vigorous and upright plants. Bushes grow 75cm/2½ft high and 60cm/2ft wide.

• 'Dearest': Spicily-fragrant, with salmon-pink or light rosy pink, camellia-like flowers. They are ideal for cutting to decorate rooms indoors, as well as growing in beds in gardens. Bushes grow 60cm/2ft high and wide.

• 'Escapade': Sweetly musk rose-scented, rosy violet flowers, but verging towards pink. They have a single, almost wild rose nature. The 82cm/32in high and 60cm/2ft wide bushes are ideal for planting in a mixed border.

• 'Pink Parfait': A North American variety, either light pink or pink with a creamy base. Bushes grow 75cm/2½ft high and 60cm/2ft wide.

• 'Queen Elizabeth': Lightly-scented, large, cyclamen-pink flowers borne in big, open trusses on vigorous bushes, 1.5m/5ft high or more high and up to 90cm/3ft wide. Often used to form a hedge.

• 'Radox Bouquet': Well-scented, rose-pink flowers, often quartered and with a cottage-garden look. They are much prized by flower arrangers. Bushes grow 90cm/3ft high and 60cm/2ft wide.

'CITY OF LEEDS' *reveals blush, salmon-pink flowers on vigorous, upright bushes.*

RED AND ROMANTIC

In the language of flowers, red roses have several meanings:
• *Red rose bud means* You are young and beautiful.
• *Fully-open red rose implies* Beauty.
• *Deep red rose tells of* Bashful shame.

FLORIBUNDAS
Red and Vermilion

THESE are dominant, dramatic colours that need to be used carefully if they are not to subdue nearby and less strong ones. There are many varieties to choose from.

• 'Anne Cocker': Large clusters of neatly-spaced, bright vermilion flowers borne on vigorous, upright bushes, 90cm/3ft high and 60cm/2ft wide.

• 'Beautiful Britain': Lightly-scented, medium-sized clusters of tomato-red flowers on vigorous, bushy plants, about 75cm/2½ft high and 60cm/2ft wide.

• 'Chorus': Slightly-scented, large, bright red flowers borne in big trusses on vigorous and bushy plants up to 75cm/2½ft high and 60cm/2ft wide.

• 'City of Belfast': Medium-sized flowers, variously described as red, velvety orange-scarlet or just scarlet. It is ideal for growing in small gardens as the bushes grow 60cm/2ft high and wide.

'BEAUTIFUL BRITAIN' *has dominant, tomato-red flowers on bushy plants.*

• 'Dusky Maiden': Fragrant, almost single, crimson flowers with deeper shading. Grow to 75cm/2½ft high and 60cm/2ft wide.

• 'Europeana': Lightly-scented, large, showy, dark red flowers borne in large trusses. Bushes grow to a height of 72cm/28in, and 60cm/2ft wide.

• 'Evelyn Fison': Lightly-scented, with large trusses of bright red, flowers. Bushes grow 75cm/2½ft high and 60cm/2ft wide.

• 'Frensham': Medium-sized, deep crimson flowers borne in large clusters on vigorous, branching bushes up to 1.2m/4ft high and 75cm/2½ft wide.

• Lilli Marlene': Lightly-scented, velvety, deep crimson flowers and coppery foliage. Bushes will grow to a height of 72cm/28in and 60cm/2ft wide.

• 'Memento': Slightly-scented, salmon-red to cherry-pink flowers borne on bushy, vigorous and upright bushes, 75cm/2½ft high and 60cm/2ft wide. The flowers are resistant to rain.

• 'Rob Roy': Lightly-scented, large, crimson-scarlet blooms borne in lax clusters on bushes growing to 90cm/3ft high and 60cm/2ft wide.

• 'Trumpeter': Lightly-scented, large, showy trusses of medium-sized, bright vermilion flowers. Sometimes they are considered to be orange-red. Bushes are 50cm/20in high and 45cm/18in wide.

• 'The Times Rose': Slightly-scented, large, dark red flowers borne in large trusses on vigorous, spreading bushes about 60cm/2ft high and 75cm/2½ft wide.

FLORIBUNDAS
Apricot, Copper and Orange

THESE are warm colours and although they do not have the dramatic colour impact of vivid red, nor the brightness of rich yellow, they are most welcome as they create a soothing ambience. They neither brighten dramatically when in strong sunlight, nor dull too much when light starts to diminish in the evening. There are many varieties to choose from, such as:

• 'Apricot Nectar': Moderately-scented, large, pale apricot petals which shade to gold at their base. They appear singly or in clusters, on plants 60cm/2ft high and wide.

• 'Anne Harkness': Lightly-scented, apricot-yellow or just apricot flowers borne in large clusters on vigorous, strong, upright bushes, up to 1.2m/4ft high and about 60cm/2ft wide.

• 'Fellowship': Scented blooms borne in widely-spaced clusters. Their colour is said to be a fusion of Spanish orange and glowing embers. It is ideal for planting in beds, as well as creating hedges, and grows up to 90cm/3ft high and 60cm/2ft wide.

• 'Geraldine': Lightly-scented, rich orange flowers borne in clusters amid spreading growth. It is ideal for planting in beds, as well as cutting to decorate rooms indoors. Bushes grow 75cm/2½ft high and 60cm/2ft wide.

• 'Iced Ginger': Lightly-scented, buff to coppery pink blooms borne in clusters on branching bushes 90cm/3ft high and 60cm/2ft high.

• 'Golden Slippers': Full, Hybrid Tea-shaped flowers with orange-flame petals with pale gold reverse. Bushes are 50cm/20in high and 45cm/18in wide.

• 'Julie Cussons': Moderately-scented, brilliant orange-salmon flowers borne on bushes about 90cm/3ft high and 60cm/2ft wide.

• 'Orange Sensation': Lightly-scented, orange-vermilion flowers borne in big clusters on bushy plants 72cm/28in high and 60cm/2ft wide.

'ORANGE SENSATION' *develops orange-vermilion flowers in large clusters.*

• 'Southampton': Clusters of slightly-ruffled, apricot-orange flowers occasionally flushed pink. It is ideal both in borders and as a cut flower for the decoration of rooms indoors. Bushes grow to about 1.2m/4ft high and 75cm/2½ft wide.

• 'Woburn Abbey': Golden orange flowers borne in large clusters on upright bushes, 90cm/3ft high and 60cm/2ft wide. Its brightness is probably derived from 'Masquerade', one of its parents.

UNUSUAL SHADES

Pink, yellow, red and orange are always popular colours, but rose enthusiasts are always searching for unusual shades or mixtures of colour. Many rose catalogues offer a medley of unusual colours.

• 'Brownie': Introduced in 1969, this rose has slightly fragrant blooms in shades of tan, edged in pink and with an attractive yellow reverse. It grows about 60cm/2ft high.

• 'Café': The sweetly-fragrant, flat, fully-double flowers are a combination of unusual colours – coffee and cream. The plants are bushy and stocky, with attractive olive-green leaves that, with the flowers, create a memorable display.

• 'Edith Holden': Also known as 'The Edwardian lady', it was introduced in 1988 and reveals russet-brown blooms with gold tints. It grows 1m/3½ft high.

• 'Jocelyn': Double, flat, dull mahogany flowers that slowly become purplish-brown. They are borne in small clusters. It grows to about 60cm/2ft high.

'ICED GINGER' *reveals buff to coppery pink blooms in clusters on branching stems.*

• 'Victoriana': Introduced in 1976, the sweetly-scented, full and rounded flowers of this Floribunda are an attractive mixture of vermilion and silver. The sturdy bushes grow to about 75cm/2½ft.

LAVENDER, PURPLE AND MAUVE

These are unusual colours in Floribundas and therefore introduce a welcome change from reds, yellows and shades of orange. They do need careful positioning to prevent them being dominated by nearby plants. Here are a few to consider:

• *'Lavender Pinocchio': Large, brownish-lavender flowers which open flat. Some experts suggest that the colour is lavender blue-grey. Bushes grow 75cm/2½ft high and 60cm/2ft wide.*

• *'Lilac Charm': Well-scented, large, lavender flowers with golden stamens on red filaments. It is free-flowering and the flowers are borne in small trusses on branching stems. Bushes grow 60cm/2ft high and wide.*

• *'Old Master': Large, deep carmine-pink flowers, edged with silvery white, borne on bushes 82cm/32in high and 60cm/18in wide.*

• *'Purple Splendour': Large, clear, glowing purple flowers borne on erect stems on bushes up to 90cm/3ft high and 60cm/2ft wide.*

• *'Shocking Blue': Scented, large, lilac-mauve flowers borne on bushy plants up to 75cm/2½ft high and 60cm/2ft wide.*

MINIATURE ROSES

THESE have a miniature stature. Few of them are taller than 38cm/15in, some only 23cm/9in, so when planting, space them about 30cm/12in apart, but only 20cm/8in for smaller varieties.

MINIATURE *roses are ideal in window-boxes. They can also be grown in troughs and placed on patios and balconies.*

WIDE RANGE OF USES

They are ideal for planting along the edges of borders, in pots on patios and in window-boxes. Those growing in pots can be taken indoors while in bloom, but they are not pot plants and must soon be returned outside, as prolonged stays in too warm positions encourages soft growth.

When grown in pots, ensure that the compost does not dry out as the roots are then soon damaged. Similarly, when grown in window-boxes, check the compost frequently during summer. Also, regularly remove dead flowers to encourage further blooms.

In winter, move miniature roses in pots and window-boxes to sheltered positions, away from strong winds. No pruning is needed at the time miniatures roses are planted. Later, the only pruning established ones need is to trim diseased and weak shoots with scissors in late winter.

MINIATURE VARIETIES

- 'Baby Masquerade': Slightly-fragrant, yellow to pink and red flowers; 45cm/1½ft high.
- 'Cinderella': White flowers tinged pink; 30cm/12in high.
- 'Darling Flame': Orange-red flowers with yellow anthers; 38cm/15in high.
- 'Easter Morning': Large, ivory-white flowers; 25cm/10in high.
- 'Green Diamond': Lime-green flowers; 30cm/12in high.
- 'New Penny': Orange-red to copper-pink; 25cm/10in high.
- 'Pour Toi': Creamy white; 30cm/12in high.

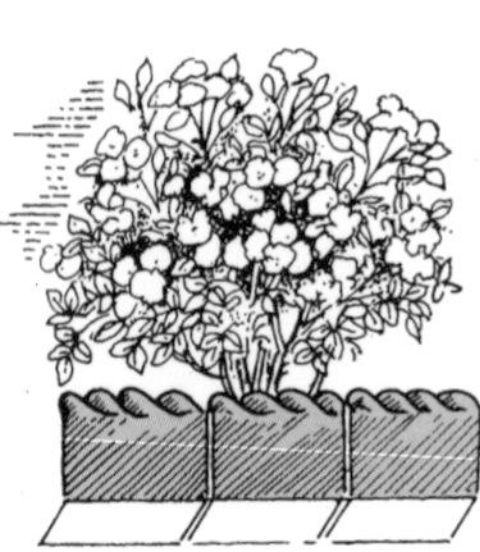

THE EDGES *of paths and patios can soon be filled with colour during summer.*

WHEN *planted in pots, miniature roses can be grown on patios and balconies.*

THEY *can be taken indoors for short periods, but avoid high temperatures.*

PATIO ROSES

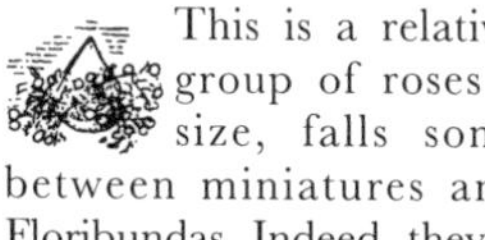

This is a relatively new group of roses and, in size, falls somewhere between miniatures and small Floribundas. Indeed, they are really small Floribundas and for this reason they are sometimes called Dwarf Cluster-flowered Bush Roses, or DCF (Patio) Bush. Most of them are between 45cm/1½ft and 60cm/2ft high, although a few only reach 38cm/15in. Their nature is more robust than that of miniature roses, with a bushy and repeat-flowering habit.

In some catalogues and books, Patio Roses have become a distinct group, while in others they are added to the Floribundas or just put with the Miniature types. Patio roses are pruned in the same way as are Floribundas, but lightly. The range of varieties is wide and includes:

- 'Anna Ford': Vivid, orange-red; 45cm/1½ft high.
- 'Bianco': White; 45cm/1½ft high.
- 'Cider Cup': Deep apricot-pink; 45cm/1½ft.
- 'Claire Rayner': Striped orange and yellow; 38cm/15in high.
- 'Conservation': Apricot-pink; 45cm/1½ft high.
- 'Drummer Boy': Deep, bright crimson; 38cm/15in high.
- 'International Herald Tribune': Violet-purple; 45cm/1½ft high.
- 'Mandarin': Deep pink, with orange-yellow centre; 38cm/15in high.
- 'Peek-a-Boo': Apricot; 45cm/1½ft high.
- 'Petite Four': Pink and white; 38cm/15in high.
- 'Ray of Sunshine': Yellow; 38cm/15in high.
- 'Red Rascal': Bright crimson; 38cm/15in high.

- 'Robin Redbreast': Red, with a pale centre; 45cm/1½ft high.
- 'Saint Boniface': Scarlet; 60cm/2ft high.
- 'Sweet Dream': Apricot-peach; 45cm/1½ft high.
- 'Wee Jock': Deep crimson; 38cm/15in high.
- 'Top Marks': Bright, vivid orange-vermilion; 38cm/15in high. Double and lightly scented.

HANGING BASKET

For an unusual display in a hanging basket, the ground-covering 'Hertfordshire' can be used. It is a member of the County Series of ground-cover shrubs and has compact growth, with masses of single, delicately-coloured, carmine-pink flowers. It spreads to about 90cm/3ft wide. Ensure that compost in the basket does not become dry.

SPECIES ROSES

THESE encompass roses which at one time could be found growing wild, alongside their natural hybrids and sports (mutations). Many of them are grown for their beautiful flowers, while some have fruits (heps or hips) with attractive shapes and colours. The flowers mostly have only five petals, but double-flowered forms have occurred as sports in the wild, while both double and semi-double forms have been selected to grow in gardens. There are many of these species (and their forms) available from garden centres and specialist nurseries, and some of them are included here:

• *Rosa californica* 'Plena': Sweetly-scented, semi-double, deep pink flowers which cascade during the latter part of early summer and into mid-summer. These are followed by red heps. Height: 1.8m/6ft. Spread:1.2–1.8m/4–6ft.

• *R. canina* 'Andersonii': Rich, brilliant pink flowers with a raspberry-drop fragrance during early summer. These are followed by red heps. Height: 1.8–2.1m/6–7ft. Spread: 1.2–1.8m/4–6ft.

ROSA CALIFORNICA *'Plena' has sweetly-scented, deep pink flowers during the latter part of early summer and into mid-summer.*

ROSA GLAUCA, *but earlier known as* R. rubrifolia, *has grey-purple leaves and cerise-pink flowers during early summer.*

• *R. ecae:* Prickly stems with fern-like leaves and bright, golden yellow flowers about 2.5cm/1in across during late spring and early summer. Height: 1.5m/5ft. Spread: 1.5m/5ft.

• *R. foetida* 'Bicolor': Known as the Austrian Copper, the shrub has a suckering nature and single flowers which are copper-red on the upperside and yellow on the reverse during late spring and early summer. Height: 1.5m/5ft. Spread: 1.2m/4ft.

• *R. glauca* (R. rubrifolia): Well-known for its grey-purple leaves and glaucous purple stems. During early summer it produces single, cerise-pink flowers about 36mm/1½in wide, in small clusters. However, it is mainly grown for its attractive foliage.

• *R. hugonis:* Arching stems with fern-like leaves and creamy yellow, 5cm/2in-wide, saucer-shaped flowers during late spring and early summer. Height: 2.1m/7ft. Spread: 1.8m/6ft.

• R. moyesii 'Geranium': Arched branches bearing brilliant red flowers about 6.5cm/2½in wide during early summer. In autumn these are followed by flask-shaped, glossy red heps. Height: 2.4m/8ft. Spread: 2.1m/7ft.

• R. x paulii 'Rosea': A vigorous, low-growing and trailing shrub with large, fragrant, fresh pink flowers with a white centre throughout summer. It is ideal for covering banks and old tree stumps. Height: 60–90cm/2–3ft. Spread: 1.8m/6ft.

• R. spinosissima (R. pimpinellifolia): This is the Scotch, Scottish or Burnet Rose, a low, thicket-forming shrub with pretty white flowers during late spring and early summer. Height: 60–90cm/2–3ft. Spread: up to 1.2m/4ft. This is the parent of the many so-called Scottish Roses.

• R. rubiginosa (earlier known as R. eglanteria): This is the well known Sweetbriar or Eglantine. The leaves are strongly fragrant, especially during warm, moist, summer evenings. The single, bright pink flowers appear during early summer. These are followed by orange-scarlet heps. Height and spread: 1.8–2.4m/6–8ft.

• R. sericea pteracantha: Small, fern-like foliage on stems noted for their extremely large, flat, red, translucent thorns. They are mahogany-red on young stems; their growth is encouraged by pruning the plant back severely in late winter. The creamy white, single flowers, up to 5cm/2in wide, appear during late spring. Height 2.4m/8ft. Spread: 1.8m/6ft.

ROSA FOETIDA *'Bicolor' has flowers that are copper-red on the upperside and yellow on the reverse.*

• R. xanthina 'Canary Bird': Prickly stems with graceful, fern-like leaves and bright, canary-yellow flowers about 42mm/1¾in wide during late spring and early summer. Height and spread: 2.1m/7ft.

• R. willmottiae: Arching stems bearing dainty, fern-like leaves and small, rosy purple flowers up to 36mm/1½in across during late spring and early summer. Small, orange-red heps. Native of North-west China, its seeds were introduced into Britain in 1904. The plant is named after the gardener and rosarian Miss Ellen Willmott.

ROSA XANTHINA *'Canary Bird' is very popular, with fern-like leaves and bright, canary-yellow flowers during late spring and into early summer.*

OLD ROSES

Alba, Bourbon, Centifolia and China Roses

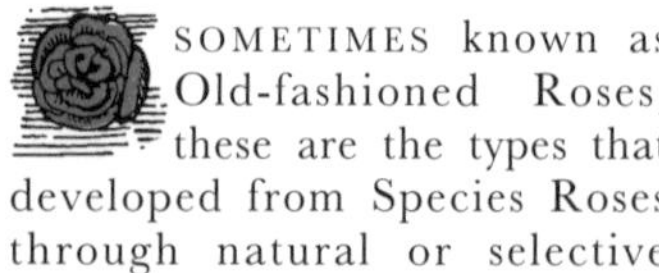

SOMETIMES known as Old-fashioned Roses, these are the types that developed from Species Roses through natural or selective hybridization, or as sports. They were especially popular during the nineteenth century and form hardy shrubs, many with unsurpassed fragrance. The flowers are mainly double, some with a carnation or camellia form, and appear during early and mid-summer, some later. A few flowers are 'quartered', and this means that the petals are in four densely-crowded groups. The centre is flat and sometimes forms an eye.

Old Roses can be grouped according to the wild species from which they developed. Occasionally, some have their origination in several groups. These roses are featured between here and page 41.

'FÉLICITÉ PARMENTIER' *(Alba) has rosette-like, fresh-pink flowers that reflex almost to a ball.*

'LOUISE ODIER' *(Bourbon) reveals warm pink flowers, softly shaded with lilac.*

ALBAS

Hardy, vigorous, upright shrubs with strong stems, a few large prickles and grey-green leaves. Flower colour ranges from white to pink and they appear during the latter part of early summer and into mid-summer.

- 'Alba Maxima' (Jacobite Rose): Fragrant, double flowers, first blush-tinted but later turning creamy white. Height: 1.8m/6ft. Spread: 1.5m/5ft.
- 'Celestial': Sweetly-scented, semi-double flowers that have golden stamens and shell-pink petals. Height: 1.8m/6ft. Spread: 1.2m/4ft.
- 'Félicité Parmentier': Fully double, rosette-like, fresh pink flowers fading to cream at their edges. Height and spread: 1.2m/4ft.
- 'Maiden's Blush': Double, blush-pink flowers that are shaped like rosettes. Height: 1.5m/5ft. Spread: 1.2m/4ft.

'FANTIN-LATOUR' *(Centifolia) has a delicate scent and blush-pink flowers that deepen to shell-pink.*

BOURBONS

These have China and Portland roses, as well as others, in their parentage. Most are strongly fragrant, with globular or cup-shaped flowers, about 7.5cm/3in wide, from early summer to autumn.

- 'Adam Messerich': Raspberry-like fragrance; semi-double, rich pink flowers. Height: 1.8m/6ft. Spread: 1.5m/5ft.
- 'Louise Odier': Scented, cup-shaped, warm pink flowers softly shaded with lilac. Height: 1.5m/5ft. Spread: 1.2m/4ft.
- 'Mme. Isaac Pereire': Fragrant, tightly-packed, cup-shaped and quartered, deep madder-pink flowers. Height: 1.5–1.8m/5–6ft. Spread: 1.2–1.5m/4–5ft.
- 'Souvenir de la Malmaison': Strongly-fragrant soft pink flowers, cupped at first but later flat and quartered. Height and spread: 90cm–1.2m/3–4ft.

CENTIFOLIAS

Provence or Cabbage Roses are descended from *R. centifolia*. The flowers, which appear in clusters during early and mid-summer, are invariably scented.

- 'Centifolia' (Cabbage Rose): Richly-fragrant, globular, clear pink flowers. Height 1.5m/5ft. Spread: 1.2m/4ft.
- 'Fantin-Latour': Delicate scent, with blush-pink flowers deepening to shell-pink. Height: 1.8m/6ft. Spread: 1.5m/5ft.
- 'Robert le Diable': Mixture of colours; parma violet, dark purple and vivid cerise, fading to grey. Height and spread: 90cm/3ft.
- 'Tour de Malakoff': Fragrant; mainly purple-magenta, fading to grey and lavender. Height: 1.8m/6ft. Spread: 1.5m/5ft.

CHINAS

These form pretty, somewhat twiggy bushes. Most are slightly tender and must not be planted in frosty positions.

- 'Hermosa': Fragrant, globular, pink flowers. Quite hardy. Height: 90cm/3ft. Spread: 60cm/2ft.
- 'Mutabilis': Flame-coloured buds open to coppery yellow, single flowers. Needs shelter. Height: 2.4m/8ft. Spread: 1.8m/6ft.
- 'Old Blush China' (Monthly Rose): Pale pink flowers over a long period. Height: 1.2m/4ft. Spread: 90cm/3ft.

'HERMOSA' *(China) produces fragrant, pink flowers that are almost globular.*

OLD ROSES
Damask, Gallica, Hybrid Musk and Hybrid Perpetual Roses

THE range of these roses is wide; many are ideal in shrub borders as well as for planting with herbaceous plants in mixed borders. They introduce height and focal points to large borders. Some, such as the Damasks, have an old heritage, while others, like Hybrid Musks, are much more recent.

'MME. HARDY' *(Damask) has cupped, white flowers with a lemon-like redolence.*

DAMASKS

Most of these have fragrant, double flowers, 7.5cm/3in wide, during early and mid-summer.

- 'La Ville de Bruxelles': Very fragrant, large, fully-double, rich pink flowers. Height: 1.5m/5ft. Spread: 1.2m/4ft.
- 'Mme. Hardy': Lemon-like fragrance, with cupped, white flowers. Height: 1.8m/6ft. Spread: 1.5m/5ft.
- 'Marie Louise': Large, intensely pink flowers that open flat, later becoming soft mauve. Height and spread: 1.2m/4ft.

GALLICAS

A large group of long-established roses. They form hardy, compact shrubs with few thorns. The flowers are richly-scented, 5–7.5cm/2–3in wide, and borne during the latter part of early summer and into mid-summer.

- 'Belle de Crécy': Richly fragrant, cerise-pink buds opening to reveal a soft parma violet. Strong, arching stems. Height: 1.2m/4ft. Spread: 90cm/3ft.
- 'Empress Joséphine': Little scent, but superb, loosely-double flowers; clear, rich pink. Height and spread: 90cm/3ft.
- 'Officinalis' (Apothecaries Rose and Red Rose of Lancaster): Large, semi-double, light crimson flowers. Golden stamens. Height and spread: 1.2m/4ft.
- 'Tuscany Superb': Fragrant, large, deep crimson flowers, fading to purple. Height: 1.5m/5ft. Spread: 90cm/3ft.

'TUSCANY SUPERB' *(Gallica) is famed for its superb, deep crimson flowers.*

'BUFF BEAUTY' *(Hybrid Musk) has warm, apricot-yellow flowers borne in large trusses.*

HYBRID MUSKS

These are derived from *Rosa moschata* (Autumn Musk Rose), but are now only distantly related.

They were mostly – but not all – bred by The Revd J. Pemberton in the early twentieth century. Flowering is mainly in early and mid-summer, and intermittently until the frosts of autumn.

- 'Ballerina': Masses of hydrangea-like heads that reveal small, single, pale pink, slightly-scented flowers. Height and spread: 1.2m/4ft.
- 'Buff Beauty': Tea-scented, with almost Hybrid Tea-like, warm apricot-yellow flowers borne in large trusses. Height and spread: 1.5m/5ft.
- 'Felicia': Aromatically-fragrant, silvery salmon-pink flowers with a Hybrid Tea shape. Height and spread: 1.5m/5ft.
- 'Penelope': Musk-scented, semi-double, rich creamy pink flowers that reveal yellow stamens. Later it develops coral-pink heps. Height and spread: 1.8m/6ft.
- 'Prosperity': Sweetly-scented, ivory-white, semi-double flowers. Height: 1.8m/6ft. Spread: 1.2m/4ft.

HYBRID PERPETUALS

These were popular in Victorian and Edwardian times and have Portland, Bourbon and China roses in their ancestry. They form vigorous shrubs, with 'cabbage-like', rounded and double flowers in clusters from early to late summer. Each flower can be up to 10cm/4in wide; most are fragrant.

- 'Baroness Rothschild': Fragrant, large and flat flowers with dark rose petals shading to shell-pink at their edge. Height: 1.5m/5ft. Spread: 90cm/3ft.
- 'Baron Girod de l'Ain': Richly-scented, large, crimson flowers with a thin, white edging. Height: 1.5m/5ft. Spread: 1.2m/4ft.
- 'Ferdinand Pichard': Richly-fragrant, with a repeat-flowering nature. The globular, pinkish-white flowers are striped purple and crimson. Height: 1.2m/4ft. Spread: 30cm/3ft.
- 'Gloire de Ducher': Fragrant, full, deep crimson flowers that slowly turn purple. Height: 1.8m/6ft. Spread: 1.2m/4ft.
- 'Reine des Violettes': Scented, quartered flowers in shades of lilac and purple. Height: 1.8m/6ft. Spread: 1.5m/5ft.

'BARONESS ROTHSCHILD' *(Hybrid Perpetual) has large, flat flowers, dark rose and shading to shell-pink.*

OLD ROSES

Hybrid Sweetbriars, Moss, Portland, Scotch and Tea Roses

THESE are further roses that are ideal in gardens. Some have a long heritage, such as the Moss types which are forms of Centifolia roses, while others, such as the Hybrid Sweetbriars, are newer and introduced mainly during the last few years of the nineteenth century.

'WILLIAM LOBB' *(Moss Rose) is also known as the Old Velvet Rose and develops dark crimson flowers that fade to a demure violet-grey.*

HYBRID SWEETBRIARS

These are also known as Penzance Briars and are the products of crosses using *Rosa rubiginosa (R. eglanteria* and commonly known as Sweetbriar and Eglantine) and *R. foetida* (Austrian Briar). The varieties are richly scented and borne in small clusters during early and mid-summer.

- 'Amy Robsart': Richly-fragrant, large, semi-double, deep rose-pink flowers and scarlet heps. Height and spread: 1.8–2.4m/6–8ft.
- 'Janet's Pride': Fragrant, single, bright cherry-pink flowers with a pale centre. Height: 1.8m/6ft high and 1.5m/5ft wide.
- 'Lady Penzance': Fragrant, single with coppery yellow tints. Height and spread: 1.8m/6ft.

'LADY PENZANCE' *(Hybrid Sweetbriar) has fragrant, coppery yellow flowers.*

MOSS ROSES

These are sports (natural mutations) derived from *Rosa centifolia* 'Muscosa', or hybrids originated from these sports. However, the mossy glands are less noticeable on the hybrids. The flowers, fragrant and up to 7.5cm/3in across, appear in early and mid-summer.

- 'Comtesse de Murinais': Fragrant, blush-pink flowers that fade to white. Height: 1.8m/6ft. Spread: 1.2m/4ft.
- 'Louis Gimard': Fragrant, large, globular flowers with light crimson petals with lilac tones. Height: 1.5m/5ft. Spread: 90cm/3ft.
- 'Maréchal Davoust': Fragrant, large, intense carmine-pink flowers that slowly become lilac and purple. Height and spread: 1.2m/4ft.
- 'William Lobb' (Old Velvet Rose): Richly-scented, dark crimson flowers that fade to a demure violet-grey. Height and spread: 1.8m/6ft.

PORTLAND ROSES

These are hardy and compact bushes, often with a suckering nature and developing Damask-type flowers up to 7.5cm/3in wide. The flowers appear mainly during the latter part of early summer and into mid-summer and frequently continue to late summer and autumn. They are borne singly or in small clusters.

- 'Comte de Chambord': Heavily-fragrant, warm pink flowers with lilac tones that become flat and quartered. Height: 1.2m/4ft. Spread: 90cm/3ft.
- 'Jacques Cartier': Strongly-scented, rich pink and rosette-shaped flowers; each is full and quartered. Height 1.2m/4ft. Spread: 90cm/3ft.
- 'Rose de Rescht': Very fragrant, purple-crimson flowers. Height: 90cm/3ft. Spread: 75cm/2½ft.

SCOTCH ROSES

These suckering, hardy and vigorous roses owe their parentage to *R. spinosissima*, widely known as the Scotch Rose, or Burnet Rose. These roses have fragrant, saucer-shaped flowers, borne singly or in small clusters during early and mid-summer.

'STANWELL PERPETUAL' *(Scotch Rose) has pale blush-pink flowers that open flat and reveal quartering.*

'COMTE DE CHAMBORD' *(Portland Rose) with warm pink flowers and lilac tones. The flowers open flat and become quartered.*

- 'Falkland': Fragrant, semi-double, pale pink flowers with their bases tinted yellow. Height and spread: 1.2m/4ft.
- 'Stanwell Perpetual': Sweetly-scented, pale blush-pink flowers that open flat to reveal quartering. They mainly appear during mid-summer and often continue throughout the rose season. Height and spread: 1.2m/4ft.
- 'William III': Fragrant, semi-double, purplish-crimson flowers fading to lilac-pink. Height and spread: 60cm/2ft.

TEA ROSES

These are not usually put with Old Roses, but as many have a long heritage they are worth including here. In 1824 a sulphur-yellow rose was introduced from China and became known as a Tea Rose. This is the originator of many superb varieties. Most are 75–90cm/2½–3ft high.

- 'Lady Hillingdon': Strongly tea-scented, with apricot-coloured flowers.
- 'Marie van Houtte': Fragrant, delicate and pretty, cream-tinged, carmine-pink flowers.

MODERN SHRUB ROSES

THESE are hardy shrubs, created from a wide range of parents, chiefly during the twentieth century. They are mainly crosses between modern bush roses and strong climbers and ramblers. The shape of their flowers is invariably modern, rather than old-fashioned and like those of Old Roses. But they have the blessing of being strong, robust and free-flowering, often intermittently throughout summer. There are many varieties and some are suggested here.

- 'Autumn Fire': Deep blood-red flowers, with darker shading, during early and mid-summer, followed by a further display in early autumn. It develops large, orange-red heps. Height and spread: 1.8m/6ft.
- 'Bloomfield Abundance': It is quite similar to 'Cecile Brunner' and bears open sprays of blush-pink flowers. Height: 1.8m/6ft. Spread: 1.5m/5ft.
- 'Cerise Bouquet': Arching stems bearing semi-double, cerise-pink, early and mid-summer flowers with the tantalizing fragrance of raspberries. Height: 2.7m/9ft. Spread: 2.4m/8ft.
- 'Fritz Nobis': Clove-scented, small, Hybrid Tea-like, fresh pink flowers especially in early summer. Attractive heps in autumn. Height and spread: 1.8m/6ft.

'FRÜHLINGSMORGEN' *reveals rose-pink flowers with yellow centres and purplish-maroon stamens during early summer.*

- 'Frühlingsanfang': Fragrant, large, single, ivory-white flowers during early and mid-summer, which are followed in autumn by maroon-red heps. Height and spread: 2.7m/9ft.
- 'Frühlingsgold': Richly fragrant, single, large, pale yellow flowers with deeper-coloured stamens during early and mid-summer. Height and spread: 2.1m/7ft.
- 'Frühlingsmorgen': Rose-pink flowers with yellow centres and purplish-maroon stamens during early summer. Sometimes a small crop appears in late summer, with large maroon-red heps in autumn. Height: 1.8m/6ft. Spread: 1.5m/5ft.
- 'Golden Wings': Fragrant, yellow flowers with mahogany-coloured stamens during summer. Height and spread: 1.2m/4ft.
- 'Jacqueline Dupré': Semi-double, blush-white flowers often 10cm/4in across almost continuously throughout summer. Height and spread: 1.8m/6ft.
- 'Magenta': Richly-scented, rosy-magenta to pale mauve flowers borne in branching sprays and spreading bushes. Height: 1.5m/5ft. Spread: 1.2m/4ft.
- 'Nevada': Semi-double, creamy white flowers with a blush tint during early and mid-summer. Further flowers appear intermittently throughout the summer. Height and spread: 2.1m/7ft.

'NEVADA' *has semi-double, creamy white flowers with a blush tint. It is one of the best-known Modern Shrub Roses.*

• 'Nymphenburg': Apple-scented double, warm salmon-pink flowers shaded cerise-pink and orange, with a yellow base to the petals. As a bonus it has large, turban-like orange-red heps in autumn. Height: 2.4m/8ft. Spread: 1.8m/6ft. Strong, arching growth.

• 'Sally Holmes': Masses of creamy white flowers in large bunches almost continuously throughout the rose season. Height and spread: 1.2m/4ft.

• 'Scarlet Fire': Single, bright scarlet flowers with golden stamens during early and mid-summer. Long-lasting, pear-shaped red heps in late summer and autumn. Height: 2.1m/7ft. Spread: 2.1–2.9m/7–9ft.

• 'Zigeunerknabe': Dark, violet-purple flowers on a prickly shrub during early summer. Height: 1.5m/5ft. Spread: 1.2m/4ft.

ENGLISH ROSES

These are roses which have been bred and introduced by David Austin Roses. They have a shrub-like habit and combine a recurrent flowering habit with a wide colour range, yet they retain the charm and fascination revealed by Old Roses. Additionally, nearly all of them have a pleasing fragrance. There are many varieties of English Rose to choose from and each year more are added.

• 'Abraham Darby': Large, deeply-cupped flowers in shades of apricot and yellow. It has the bonus of a rich, fruit-like fragrance. Flowering begins in early summer and continues for the rest of the season. Height and spread: 1.5m/5ft.

• 'Constance Spry': Clear pink flowers with myrrh-like fragrance during summer. Height and spread: 1.8–2.1m/6–7ft.

• 'Graham Thomas': Rich, pure yellow flowers with a cupped formation and a refreshing Tea Rose fragrance. Flowering is almost continual throughout summer. Height and spread: 1.2m/4ft.

• 'Heritage': Soft pink flowers with a lemon-like fragrance; repeat-flowering throughout summer. Height and spread: 1.2m/4ft.

• 'The Countryman': Clear pink flowers with an Old Rose fragrance. It flowers twice during summer, each with a good crop. Height: 90cm/3ft. Spread: 1m/3½ft.

• 'Red Coat': Large, single, crimson-scarlet flowers continuously through the rose season. Height: 1.5m/5ft. Spread: 1.2m/4ft.

• 'Shropshire Lass': Delicate flesh-pink, fading to white, but only once during the season. Height: 2.4m/8ft. Spread: 1.8m/6ft.

• 'Winchester Cathedral': White flowers at intervals throughout summer. Height and spread: 1.2m/4ft. Bushy growth.

CLIMBERS

THESE have a more permanent framework than ramblers, and their flowers, when compared with those of ramblers, are larger and borne singly or in small clusters. And they generally have the ability of repeat flowering after their first flush of flowers.

Climbers can be arranged into four main groups, according to their parentage, although there are some that do not neatly fit into any of these groups. And, of course, there are also Modern Climbers (see opposite page).

'ÉTOILE DE HOLLANDE, CLIMBING', *has strongly fragrant, deep crimson flowers.*

CLIMBING BOURBONS

Hardy, with flowers that reveal a beautiful Old Rose appearance. They also often have a repeat-flowering nature.

- 'Blairi No. 2': Not an exciting name but a beautiful rose, deep pink at the centre and paling at its edge. Only one good flush of flowers a year. Height 4.5m/15ft.
- 'Kathleen Harrop': Fragrant and soft-pink; almost perpetual flowers in season. This rose is a sport of 'Zéphirine Drouhin', but slightly less vigorous and with a more attractive colour. Height: 3.6m/12ft.

CLIMBERS *are superb for clothing walls, but first secure a trellis to the wall to support them. The trellis should be positioned slightly away from the wall, to allow stems to pass behind it.*

CLIMBING HYBRID TEAS

These are usually sports of bush varieties, with flowers that reveal a Hybrid Tea nature.

- 'Allen Chandler': Fragrant, large, semi-double, bright crimson flowers with golden yellow stamens. Height: 4.5m/15ft.
- 'Étoile de Hollande, Climbing': Strongly fragrant and deep crimson. Height: 5.4m/18ft.
- 'Guinée': Strongly fragrant and deep, velvety crimson. Golden stamens. Height: 4.5m/15ft.
- 'Mrs. Sam McGredy, Climbing': Coppery-orange flowers flushed with scarlet. Height: 4.5m/15ft.
- 'Ophelia, Climbing': Richly-fragrant, with pale blush-pink buds. Height: 3.6m/12ft.
- 'Shot Silk, Climbing': Scented and in shades of cerise-pink with orange-scarlet and yellow. Height: 5.4m/18ft.
- 'Souvenir de Claudius Denoyel': Richly-fragrant and bright crimson. Height: 5.4m/18ft.
- 'Sutter's Gold, Climbing': Fragrant with buds flushed gold and peach. Height 3.6m/12ft.

CLIMBING TEA ROSES

These have flowers slightly resembling those of Hybrid Tea types, but perhaps slightly nearer to Noisettes (see below). A warm position is essential.

- 'Lady Hillingdon, Climbing': Richly Tea Rose-scented, apricot-yellow flowers. Height: 4.5m/15ft.
- 'Mrs Herbert Stevens, Climbing': Tea Rose-scented, white flowers tinged green. Height: 6m/20ft.
- 'Paul Lede': Tea Rose-fragrant, yellow-buff flowers flushed carmine at the centre. Height: 3.6m/12ft. Very free-flowerng.
- 'Sombreuil, Climbing': Superbly Tea Rose-scented, creamy white flowers. Height: 3.6m/12ft.

'NEW DAWN' *is a Modern Climber with silvery blush-pink flowers.*

'MERMAID' *has large, single, yellow flowers with a delicate fragrance. It grows up to 9m/30ft high.*

NOISETTE CLIMBERS

Small and rosette-shaped blooms, on plants that have a repeat-flowering nature. A warm, sunny wall is essential.

- 'Aimée Vibert': Musk-fragrant, small, double, pure white flowers. Height: 4.5m/15ft.
- 'Alister Stella Gray': Double, rosette-shaped, yellow flowers, with a repeat-flowering nature. Height: 4.5m/15ft.
- 'Blush Noisette': Richly clove-scented, semi-double and cup-shaped, lilac-pink flowers. Height: 4.5m/15ft.
- 'Céline Forestier': Tea Rose-scented, pale yellow flowers. Height, 2.4m/8ft.
- 'Gloire de Dijon' (Old Glory Rose): Richly fragrant, large, buff-yellow flowers often tinted gold and pink. Height 4.5m/15ft.

MODERN CLIMBERS

Relatively new; flowers resemble those of Hybrid Teas.

- *'Breath of Life': Fragrant and apricot-pink. Height: 2.4m/8ft.*
- *'Danse du Feu': Semi-double and orange-scarlet. Height: 3m/10ft.*
- *'Golden Showers': Scented, semi-double, golden yellow flowers fading to cream. Height: 3m/10ft.*
- *'New Dawn': Fruity fragrance and silvery blush-pink. Height: 3m/10ft.*
- *'Pink Perpétué': Bright rose-pink. Height 4.5m/15ft.*

RAMBLERS

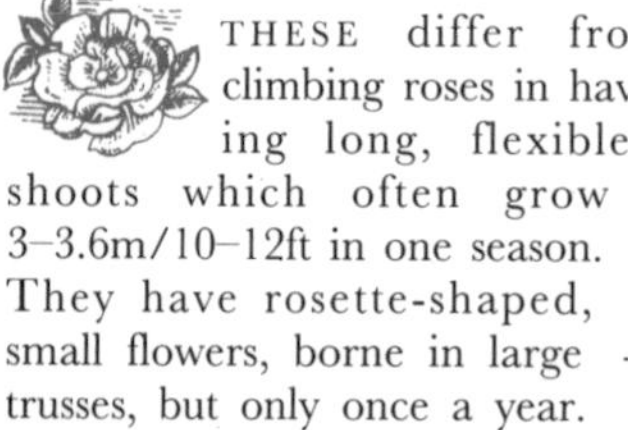

THESE differ from climbing roses in having long, flexible shoots which often grow 3–3.6m/10–12ft in one season. They have rosette-shaped, small flowers, borne in large trusses, but only once a year. Their growth is vigorous but graceful. They are ideal for clothing arches and pergolas, or rambling through bushes and into trees.

Ramblers can be grouped according to their parentage, but there are some with various origins and a few of these are described on the opposite page (other ramblers).

'ALBERTINE' *is one of the most popular ramblers, with fragrant flowers that open to reveal coppery pink petals.*

MULTIFLORA HYBRIDS

These have small flowers borne in large trusses and on stiff growths.

- 'Bleu Magenta': Violet-crimson flowers fading to parma violet and grey. Height 4.5m/15ft.
- 'Bobbie James': Fragrant, semi-double, creamy white flowers borne in large trusses. Height: 9m/30ft.
- 'Goldfinch': Well-scented, yolk-yellow flowers fading to soft, milky white. Height 3m/10ft.
- 'Rambling Rector': Superbly-fragrant, semi-double, small creamy white flowers. Dense, twiggy growth. Height: 6m/20ft.
- 'Veilchenblau': Orange-scented, dark magenta flowers fading to lilac. Height: 4.5m/15ft.
- 'Violette': Crimson-purple flowers fading to maroon. It has the bonus of golden stamens. Height: 4.5m/15ft.

SEMPERVIRENS HYBRIDS

These hybrid roses are graceful, with long, slender but strong stems. The small flowers are borne in sprays.

- 'Adeläide d'Orléans': Primrose-scented, semi-double, creamy - white flowers. Height: 4.5m/15ft.
- 'Félicité et Perpétué': Primrose-scented, pompon-like, creamy white flowers. The buds are tinted pink. Height 6m/20ft.
- 'Princess Louise': Slightly-fragrant, soft pink buds which open to reveal creamy blush flowers. Height: 3.6m/12ft.

WICHURAIANA HYBRIDS

This group includes the majority of ramblers; they are graceful with large flowers in elegant sprays.

- 'Albéric Barbier': Fruitily fragrant, fully-double, creamy white flowers about 7.5cm/3in wide. Height: 7.5m/25ft.
- 'Albertine': Richly-fragrant, with reddish-salmon buds which open to reveal coppery pink flowers. Height: 6m/20ft.

• 'American Pillar': Well-known rambler, with single, bright pink flowers. Height 4.5m/15ft.
• 'Crimson Shower': Superb rambler, with bright crimson flowers from mid-summer to early autumn. Height 4.5m/15ft.
• 'Francois Juranville': Apple-like fragrance and double, coral-pink flowers. They open flat and reveal yellow bases to the petals. Height 7.5m/25ft.
• 'Léontine Gervais': Graceful climber with pink flowers tinged with orange and copper. Height: 7.5m/25ft.
• 'Paul Transon': Apple-like fragrance to the medium-sized, coppery-orange flowers borne in small clusters. Usually, there is repeat flowering in early autumn. Height: 4.5m/15ft.
• 'René André': Apple-like fragrance to the small, cupped, soft apricot-yellow flowers which are flushed in pink and borne on trailing stems. Height: 6m/20ft.
• 'Sander's White': Fragrant, small, semi-double, pure white flowers borne on trailing stems. Height: 5.4m/18ft.

'AMERICAN PILLAR' *is vigorous, with single, bright pink flowers. It is well-known and popular.*

'VEICHENBLAU' *produces bunches of dark magenta flowers that fade to lilac. The stems do not have thorns.*

OTHER RAMBLERS

In addition to ramblers which derive from Multiflora, Sempervirens and Wichuraiana sources, there are several others. Included in them are:
• *'Kew Rambler': Derived from* Rosa soulieana, *it has strongly-fragrant, single, rose-pink flowers with a white eye. Height: 5.4m/18ft.*
• *'Mme. Sancy de Parabère': A slightly-fragrant Boursault type, with 13cm/5in wide, soft pink flowers. Height: 4.5m/15ft.*
• *'Paul's Himalayan Musk': A popular rambler, with sprays of small, blush-pink flowers. It is vigorous and ideal for climbing into trees. Height: 9m/30ft.*
• *'The Garland': A richly orange-scented cross between* Rosa moschata *and* R. multiflora. *It develops small, creamy salmon flowers. Height: 4.5m/15ft.*
• *'Weetwood': Pendulous sprays of pink flowers, each about 6.5cm/2½in wide. Height: 7.5m/25ft.*

PILLARS, TREES AND SCREENS

THERE are many roses that vigorously clamber into trees. Some are more than 9m/30ft high, while others have a shorter stature and are suitable for creating feasts of colour 2.4–3m/8–10ft high.

Establishing a new rose around the base of a tree is neither easy nor rapid. This is because soil around a tree is invariably impoverished and dry; the roots of trees absorb all nutrients and the canopy of leaves prevents soil close to the trunk becoming moist. Therefore, dig a large hole about 45cm/18in deep and 1m/3½ft from the tree and fill it with a mixture of decomposed compost and good soil. Plant the rose's roots in it and keep them moist, especially during the first season. Additionally, feed it two or three times every year, as the tree will be in competition with the rose.

'GOLDEN SHOWERS' *(Modern Climber) is ideal as a pillar rose, about 3m/10ft high and with blush-pink flowers.*

COVERING TREES

Old trees can be transformed by training climbers to wander through their branches. No regular pruning is needed and once established there is little to do but to feed them a couple of times a year, during early and mid-spring. The range of suitable roses is wide and they do not have to be exceptionally vigorous. Indeed, many of them are only 3m/10ft high but well able to clothe a small tree with colour. Roses to consider include:

- 'Awakening': Blush; 3–3.6m/10–12ft; climber.
- 'Bobby James': Creamy white; 9m/30ft; rambler.
- 'Blush Rambler': Apple blossom-pink; 2.7m/9ft; rambler.
- 'Cécile Brunner, Climbing': Light pink; 3.6m/12ft; climber.
- 'Dr. W. Van Fleet': Soft pink; 6m/20ft; rambler.
- 'Emily Gray': Butter-yellow; 4.5m/15ft; rambler.
- 'Félicité et Perpétué': Creamy white; 6m/20ft; rambler.
- 'Francis E. Lester': White, tinted blush; 4.5m/15ft; rambler.
- 'Leverkusen': Lemon-yellow; 3m/10ft; climber.
- 'Meg': Pink with an apricot centre; 3–3.6m/10–12ft, climber.
- 'Mme. Grégoire Staechelin': Rosy carmine-pink; 6m/20ft; climber.
- 'Paul's Himalayan Musk': Blush-pink; 9m/30ft; rambler.
- 'Scharlachglut': Bright red; 3m/10ft; shrub rose.
- 'Sympathie': Rich, blood-red; 4.5m/15ft; climber.
- 'Veilchenblau': Dark magenta and fading to lilac; 4.5m/15ft; rambler.
- 'Wedding Day': Creamy-white to blush; 7.5m/25ft; rambler.

'WHITE COCKADE' *(Modern Climber) is a pillar rose, about 2.1m/7ft high with pure white, Hybrid Tea-like flowers.*

PILLAR ROSES

These are less vigorous than the varieties mainly used to clamber into trees: they are usually 2.4–3m/8–10ft high, occasionally slightly higher. They have a repeat-flowering nature.

The range of varieties is wide:

- 'Aloha' (Modern Shrub Rose): Clear pink and repeat-flowering.
- 'Bantry Bay' (Climber): Deep pink and semi-double.
- 'Compassion' (Modern Climber): Salmon-pink, petals tinted apricot-orange.
- 'Dreaming Spires' (Climber): Yellow and scented.
- 'Handel' (Modern Climber): Creamy blush, edged pink.
- 'Phyllis Bide' (Rambler): Yellow, flushed salmon-pink.
- 'Pink Perpétué' (Modern Climber): Bright rose-pink.
- 'La Reine Victoria' (Bourbon Shrub): Shell-pink.

IMPENETRABLE BARRIERS

Some roses create dense barriers that are ideal for keeping out stray animals and to provide privacy. Suitable roses include:

- 'Blanc Double de Coubert' (Rugosa): Large, semi-double, pure-white flowers throughout most of summer. Height: 1.8m/6ft. Spread: 1.5m/5ft.
- 'Constance Spry' (English Rose): Strongly myrrh-fragrant, clear pink flowers. Height and spread: 1.8–2.1m/6–7ft.
- 'Frühlingsgold' (Modern Shrub Rose): Fragrant and pale yellow. Height and spread: 2.1m/7ft.
- 'Nevada' (Modern Shrub Rose): Semi-double and creamy white. Height and spread: 2.1m/7ft.
- *Rosa* x *cantabrigiensis* (Hybrid): Pale yellow flowers. Height and spread: 3m/10ft.
- 'Roseraie de l'Hay (Rugosa): Scented and rich, wine-red. Height and spread: 2.1m/7ft.

CLIMBERS FOR COLD WALLS

Roses are never fully happy when planted against a north-facing wall. Apart from low temperatures and freezing winds (which they can usually tolerate when in their dormant state), in summer they tend to be drawn towards the light. However, there are a few climbers and ramblers that tolerate such conditions.

- *'Albéric Barbier' (rambler).*
- *'Félicité et Perpétué' (rambler).*
- *'Mme. Grégoire Staechelin' (climber).*
- *'Mme. Plantier' (Alba climber).*
- *'Morning Jewel' (climber).*
- *'New Dawn' (Modern climber).*
- *'Zéphirine Drouhin' (Bourbon climber).*

STANDARDS AND WEEPING STANDARDS

THESE are superb for creating 'height' in rose beds and as centre-pieces in lawns. There are several types of standard roses, from low and small ones in pots to those 1.5–1.8m/5–6ft tall.

STANDARD ROSES

These are budded by nurserymen on established root-stocks, 1m/39in above the ground, where they form heads 1.5m–1.8m/5–6ft high. Strong stakes are essential. Both Hybrid Tea and Floribunda varieties are used.

- Hybrid Tea varieties to choose include: 'Just Joey' (copper-orange), 'Ruby Wedding' (ruby-red), 'Silver Wedding' (creamy white), 'Simba' (yellow), 'Tequila Sunrise' (yellow, edged scarlet).
- Floribunda varieties include 'Amber Queen' (amber-yellow), 'Golden Wedding' (yellow), 'Iceberg' (white) and 'Intrigue' (dark red).

DOUBLE OR SINGLE-BUDDED

The best standards have two – sometimes three – buds of the varietal part budded on to the top of root-stocks. This ensures stems are evenly spaced around the top. It is possible that one of these buds grows more strongly than the other. If this happens, prune back the weaker shoot harder than the strong one.

Where only one bud has been used – and it is best not to buy such a plant – it is essential initially to cut back the subsequent shoots to three or four eyes. If this task is neglected, the head will be lop-sided.

'TEQUILA SUNRISE' *(Hybrid Tea) is often used to create standard roses. It has yellow blooms edged in scarlet.*

HALF-STANDARD ROSES

These have a lower stature than full standards; varieties are budded on to root-stocks, 75cm/2½ft above the ground, where they form heads 1.3–1.6m/4½–5½ft high.

- Hybrid Tea varieties include: 'Paul Shirville' (soft salmon-pink), 'Royal William' (deep red) and 'Savoy Hotel' (light pink).
- Floribunda types include: 'Amber Queen' (amber-yellow), 'Golden Years' (golden), and 'Margaret Merril' (blush-white).

PATIO STANDARDS

The varietal parts are budded on root-stocks, 75cm/2½ft above ground level, and form dense, rounded heads. They become packed with flowers through much of summer and into autumn and create dominant features. They are ideal when close to patios and for growing in large pots.

- Varieties to consider include: 'Cider Cup' (peach), 'Muriel' (pink), 'Red Rascal' (red) and 'Sweet Magic' (orange).

MINIATURE STANDARDS
These are even smaller than patio roses, and are budded onto root-stocks 50cm/20in above the ground. When the head matures, its top is about 90cm/3ft tall. These are ideal for growing in large pots on patios. Avoid positions in strong draughts.

• Varieties include: 'Baby Masquerade' (bicolor), 'Colibri '79' (apricot and orange), 'Orange Sunblaze' (scarlet) and 'Pink Sunblaze' (pink).

WEEPING STANDARDS
These are well-known for their beautiful outline, often with stems cascading and reaching nearly to the ground. To be fully appreciated, a weeping standard is best planted as a feature on a lawn.

Weeping standards are created by budding the varietal part on to a rootstock, about 130cm/51in above the ground. When mature, the head is then 1.5–1.8m/5–6ft high, with stems trailing evenly from around the top.

• Mainly rambler varieties are used to create a cascading outline: 'Albéric Barbier' (cream), 'Crimson Showers' (red), 'Débutante' (clear rose-pink), 'Francois Juranville' (salmon-pink), 'Goldfinch' (yellow, fading to white), 'Princess Louise' (creamy blush) and 'Sander's White' (white).

• Climbing roses with arching stems are also used and these include: 'Félicité et Perpétué' (white) and 'New Dawn' (silvery blush-pink; a Modern Climber).

'AMBER QUEEN' *(Floribunda) creates spectacular standard roses. It bears large clusters of amber-yellow blooms.*

SHRUBBY STANDARDS
These involve the budding of Shrub Roses on to root-stocks, 1m/39in above ground level.

• Varieties include: 'Ballerina' (light pink), 'Canary Bird' (golden yellow) and 'Bonica' (pink).

GROUND-COVER STANDARDS
Ground-cover roses are budded on root-stocks, 1m/39in high.

• Suitable varieties include: 'Gwent' (yellow), 'Hertfordshire' (carmine), 'Kent' (white) and 'Surrey' (pink).

SMALL TRAILING STANDARDS
These require less room than full standards and are budded on root-stocks 1m/39in high. They mature to 1.3m/4½ft.

• Varieties include 'Nozomi' (blush) and 'Suma' (red).

WEEPING ROSE TRAINERS

To ensure that a weeping standard creates an even arrangement of stems, secure a rose trainer to the top of its stake. These are formed of plastic-coated wire and are available in several sizes: 60cm/2ft, 75cm/2½ft and 90cm/3ft wide.

HEDGES

ROSES create superb hedges, whether along a perimeter or within a garden. However, unlike traditional hedging plants, such as Yew and Privet, roses are deciduous and therefore during winter have bare, leafless stems. For this reason, if privacy is desired throughout the year they are not suitable. Do not expect to be able to form a rigid outline, with a uniform height and width. Rather, they have a lax and informal nature.

'LITTLE WHITE PET' *forms a low hedge packed with white flowers.*

PLANTING A ROSE HEDGE

Plant bare-rooted rose bushes during their dormant period, from late autumn to late winter. Dig out a trench and add garden compost or manure: use the spacings suggested for each group. Plant firmly and keep the soil moist. In spring, cut back the plants hard to encourage bushiness.

LOW HEDGES

These are up to 75cm/2½ft high and formed of Miniature, Patio, Dwarf Polyantha and short-growing Floribundas. They are planted in a single row, with 30–38cm/12–15in between the plants. Ensure the foliage overlaps. Varieties include: 'Little White Pet' (white), 'Marlena' (scarlet-crimson) and 'The Fairy' (rose-pink).

MEDIUM-HEIGHT HEDGES

These range from 75cm/2½ft to 1.5m/5ft high and are planted 45cm/1½ft apart. To create a dense, thick hedge, plant them in two rows, staggered and about 45cm/1½ft apart.

Varieties to consider include: 'Celestial' (shell-pink), 'Iceberg' (white) and 'Masquerade' (yellow, red and pink).

TALL HEDGES

These grow 1.5m/5ft to 2.1m/7ft high and are best reserved for boundaries. Plant them 75–90cm/2½–3ft apart. Varieties include 'Felicia' (silvery pink), 'Penelope' (pink, flushed apricot) and 'Queen Elizabeth' (pink).

'CELESTIAL', *an Alba type, forms a medium-height hedge, with sweetly-scented, shell-pink flowers.*

GROUND COVER

GROWING roses to form an attractive covering of the soil is increasing in popularity. However, do not expect them to form a weed-smothering blanket of stems, leaves and flowers in the same way as many other ground-cover plants. Instead, they produce a magnificent blanket of colour. For this reason, never plant them in soil plagued with perennial weeds, as they will continue to grow and be difficult to eradicate. Always dig out perennial weeds before planting roses.

These roses are superb for covering steep banks (where it would be difficult to mow grass), masking manhole covers, and creating colourful edges to rose beds.

'SURREY', *one of the County Series of ground-cover plants, has rich, reddish-pink, single flowers.*

MODERN SHRUB ROSES

These are a relatively recent introduction and usually develop large trusses of flowers. They are easily grown and many have a repeat-flowering nature, others flower once but over a long period. Varieties include: 'Max Graf' (apple-scented and pink), 'Nozomi' (pearly pink to white), 'Partridge' (white), 'Rosy Cushion' (pink), 'Snow Carpet' (white).

'PARTRIDGE', *a Modern Shrub Rose, has low, prostrate growth and forms a wide carpet, often 2.4m/8ft across, of single, white flowers.*

Further Modern Shrub Roses that cover the ground include: 'Raubritter' (pink), 'Running Maid' (deep pink) and 'Scintillation' (semi-double, bluish-pink).

COUNTY SERIES

These are popular and create a mass of flowers from the latter part of early summer to the middle of autumn. Most of them grow between 30cm/12in and 45cm/18in high, and with a 60cm/2ft to 1.2m/4ft spread. Varieties to consider include:

- 'Avon': Pearly white.
- 'Essex': Rich reddish-pink.
- 'Gwent': Bright lemon-yellow.
- 'Hampshire': Glowing scarlet.
- 'Hertfordshire': Carmine-pink.
- 'Norfolk': Bright yellow.
- 'Suffolk': Bright scarlet.
- 'Warwickshire': Deep rosy red.
- 'Wiltshire': Deep rosy pink.

FRAGRANCE

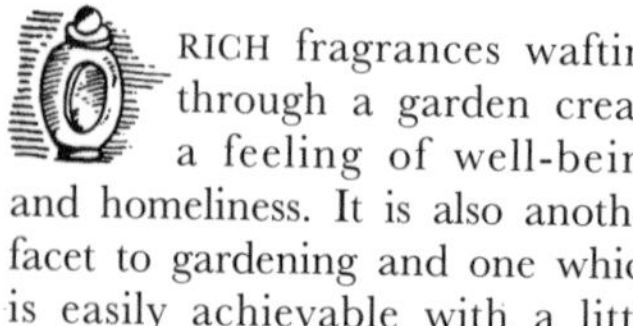

RICH fragrances wafting through a garden create a feeling of well-being and homeliness. It is also another facet to gardening and one which is easily achievable with a little planning. And of all garden plants, roses reveal some of the most varied scents.

SHRUB ROSES

These, like the climbers and ramblers featured on the opposite page, are frequently rich in unusual fragrances.

- Banana: *Rosa soulieana* (Species) reveals white flowers in sprays.
- Clove: *Rosa* x *paulii* has white flowers with golden stamens. Also, *R.* x *paulii rosea*, with single, pink flowers.
- Clover: 'Fritz Nobis' (Modern Shrub Rose) reveals fresh pink flowers with darker shading.
- Musk: 'Day Break' (Hybrid Musk) with rich yellow buds opening to yellow flowers with golden stamens. 'Penelope' (Hybrid Musk) bearing large clusters of creamy pink flowers.
- Myrrh: 'Magenta' (listed as a Modern Shrub Rose or Hybrid Musk) with rosy magenta to pale mauve flowers, and said to have the soft colouring of Old Roses.
- Orange: 'Callisto' (Hybrid Musk) with rich creamy yellow flowers.
- Raspberry: 'Adam Masserich' (Bourbon Rose) with large, semi-double, rich pink flowers. 'Cerise Bouquet' (Modern Shrub Rose) with cerise-pink, semi-double flowers. 'Great Western' (Bourbon Rose) with rich crimson-purple flowers with maroon shading. 'Kathleen Harrop' (Bourbon Rose) with clear pink flowers, showing light crimson on the reverse.
- Raspberry-drop: *Rosa canina* 'Andersonii' (Species type) with large, intense deep pink flowers.
- Sweet and apple-like: 'Nymphenburg' (Modern Shrub Rose) with fully-double, warm salmon-pink flowers shaded with cerise and orange-yellow.
- Sweet and lemony: 'Mme. Hardy' (Damask Rose). White flowers, copper at first.
- Sweet Pea: 'Vanity' (Hybrid Musk) with single, deep pink flowers borne in large, lax trusses.

'DUTCH GOLD', *(Hybrid Tea)* *has a vigorous and upright nature, with large golden flowers.*

SHELTERED POSITIONS

Choose a warm, wind-sheltered position close to a path, so that fragrances can be easily appreciated. Take care that thorn-covered stems cannot cause harm to faces, and especially to eyes.

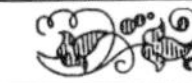

HYBRID TEAS

Many of these bush-type roses have a sweet fragrance and some, such as 'Alec's Red', are ideal for cutting to decorate rooms.

- White and cream: 'Evening Star' and 'Polar Star'.
- Lilac and mauve: 'Blue Parfum'.
- Pink: 'Double Delight', 'Mary Donaldson', 'My Choice', 'Ophelia', 'Paul Shirville' and 'Royal Highness'.
- Red: 'Alec's Red', 'Barkarole', 'Deep Secret', 'Ena Harkness', 'Ernest H. Morse', 'Fragrant Cloud', 'Royal William' and 'Wendy Cussons'.
- Yellow: 'Champion', 'Dutch Gold' and 'Pot o' Gold'.
- Orange and blends: 'Just Joey' and 'Whisky Mac'.

FLORIBUNDA ROSES

Like Hybrid Teas, these are also rich in fragrance and are ideal for drenching beds and borders in scent as well as colour.

- White and cream: 'Iceberg' and 'Margaret Merril'.
- Pink: 'Champion Cocktail', 'Dearest', 'Harry Edland', 'Radox Bouquet', 'Scented Air', 'The Fisherman's Cottage' and 'Valentine Heart'.
- Red: 'Dusky Maiden' and 'Geranium Red'.
- Yellow: 'Arthur Bell', 'Korresia' and 'Mountbatten'.
- Orange and blends: 'Daylight', 'Elizabeth of Glamis', 'Fragrant Delight' and 'Iced Ginger'.

DWARF POLYANTHAS

These are one of the parents of Floribundas, with small rambler-type flowers in closely-packed clusters. They flower over a long period and some are richly scented.

- 'Katharina Zeimet': white.
- 'Nathalie Nypels': rose pink.
- 'Yvonne Rabier': white.

'ALEC'S RED' *(Hybrid Tea) develops large, cherry-red flowers and strong shoots bearing dark green and glossy leaves.*

RAMBLERS AND CLIMBERS

Some ramblers and climbers have unusual fragrances, such as:

- *Apple: 'François Juranville' (R: coral-pink); 'Paul Transon' (R: coppery orange) and 'René André' (R: soft apricot-yellow).*
- *Cloves: 'Blush Noisette' (C: semi-double and lilac-pink).*
- *Fruity: 'Leander' (S/C: a warm, deep apricot).*
- *Musk: 'Paul's Himalayan Musk' (R: blush-pink).*
- *Myrrh: 'Constance Spry' (S/C: clear pink) and 'Cressida' (S/C: apricot-pink).*
- *Orange: 'The Garland' (R: creamy salmon) and 'Veilchenblau' (R: magenta, fading to lilac).*
- *Paeony: 'Gerbe Rose' (R: soft pink tinted cream).*
- *Primrose: 'Adelaïde d'Orléans' (R: creamy white) and 'Félicité et Perpétué' (R: creamy white).*
- *Sweet Pea: 'Mme Gregoire Staechelin' (C: glowing pink).*

[Note: R = Rambler: C = Climber: S/C = Shrub/climber]

COMPANION PLANTING

IN earlier years, roses were usually grown in beds on their own, either in a single colour or mixed. Today, planting roses – whether bush types, climbers, ramblers or those with a shrub-like nature – in attractive groups with other plants has become an increasing and fascinating trend. There are many attractive combinations to choose from and a few of these eye-catching displays are suggested here.

BUSH ROSES

These include Hybrid Tea and Floribunda Roses.

• The vigorous Floribunda 'Queen Elizabeth', 1.5m/5ft high or more and spreading to 90cm/3ft, looks superb when planted against a background of the Common Yew *(Taxus baccata)*. The cyclamen-pink flowers of the rose are framed by the dark green leaves of Yew. Additionally, plant *Lavandula* 'Hidcote' (deep, blue-purple flowers) and Rosemary *(Rosmarinus officinalis* 'Severn Sea') in front of the rose.

• The buttercup yellow Floribunda 'Allgold' forms a pleasing combination with the deep lavender flowers of *Clematis* 'Countess of Lovelace'. It flowers from early summer to autumn, with double-flowered forms in summer, and single flowers in late summer and into autumn.

• Plant the pale yellow Hybrid Tea 'Grandpa Dickson', which grows about 75cm/2½ft high, against a background of the richly dark purple leaves of *Berberis thunbergii* 'Atropurpurea'. The yellow-green Flowering Tobacco plant *Nicotiana alata* 'Lime Green' adds a further colour when planted in front of the rose.

• Underplant white-flowered bush roses with the Foam Flower *(Tiarella cordifolia)*, which has pale to mid-green, maple-like leaves with the bonus of creamy white flowers in early summer.

• Plant three red-flowered standard roses in a round bed planted with bright yellow bush roses. Plant white-flowered Sweet Alyssum around the edge.

'QUEEN ELIZABETH', *a Floribunda type, looks superb when planted against a dark green background formed by the Common Yew.*

PLANT *lavender and Rosemary in front of the cyclamen-pink flowers of 'Queen Elizabeth', which forms a tall background.*

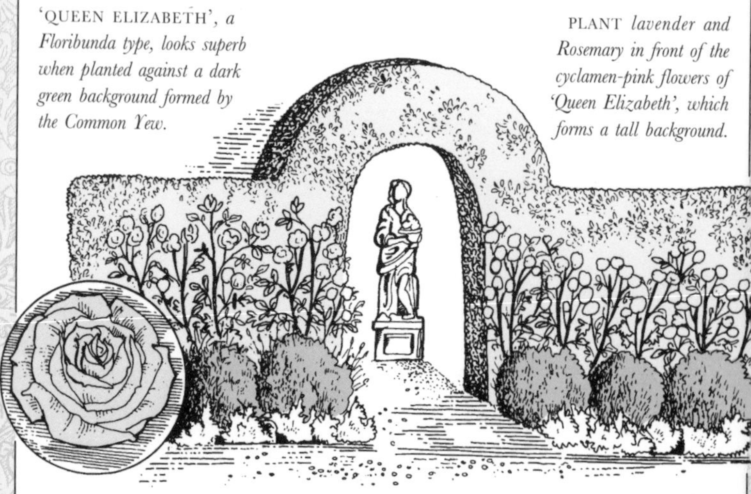

SHRUB ROSES

These include a wide range of roses of many different types.

• The Alba Rose 'Königin von Danemark' ('Queen of Denmark'), about 1.5m/5ft high and 1.2m/4ft wide, has deep pink flowers which look superb when planted against the slightly weeping silver-leaved *Pyrus salicifolia* 'Pendula'.

• The Gallica Rose 'Tuscany Superb', which grows to about 1.2m/4ft high, has dark maroon-crimson flowers with golden stamens. It forms an attractive combination with *Ipomoea violacea* (also known as *I. tricolor* and *I. rubro-caerulea*), which develops reddish-purple to blue flowers.

• The Modern Shrub Rose 'Nevada' has semi-double, creamy white flowers about 10cm/4in wide which create a magnificent background for the blue-flowered forms of delphinium and campanula, with their many and very varied shapes.

• The Damask Rose 'Mme Hardy' reveals beautiful white flowers. It grows 1.8m/6ft high and 1.5m/5ft wide and creates an ideal background for pink and demure red flowers. The pale pink Old-fashioned Pink 'Inchmery' and the herbaceous *Geranium endressii*, which has several pink varieties, are superb companions.

• The Hybrid Musk 'Buff Beauty' produces warm, apricot-yellow flowers in large trusses. It looks especially good when surrounded with a sea of light blue, white and light orange flowers. These could be formed of Catmint (*Nepeta* x *faasenii*) and the Oriental Poppy *Papaver orientale* 'Perry's White'.

• The New English Rose 'Constance Spry' has magnificent pink flowers and grows 1.8–2.1m/6–8ft high and wide. It can be highlighted by planting silver-leaved plants around it.

CLIMBERS AND RAMBLERS

These are ideal for clothing walls, tumbling over trellises and pergolas, or clambering into trees.

• The climber 'Helen Knight' has dainty, fern-like leaves and yellow flowers during early summer. These combine well with the pure white flowers of *Clematis montana*. For a softer-coloured combination, use the form 'Elizabeth', with slightly-fragrant, pale pink flowers. Choose a warm, wind-sheltered and sun-blessed wall on which to grow them.

'BOBBIE JAMES' *is ideal for climbing into trees, where it creates a mass of creamy white flowers. They harmonize well with blue flowers: set them around its base.*

• Rambler 'Bobbie James', with semi-double, creamy white flowers grows up to 9m/30ft high and is ideal for clambering up trees and over pergolas. Plant dominant groups of blue flowers, such as Catmint, around it to form a colour contrast.

• Modern Climber 'New Dawn', with silvery blush-pink flowers, grows about 3m/10ft high. Plant the light blue and vigorous Clematis 'Perle d'Azure' to sprawl and clamber among it. Flowering is from early to late summer.

PESTS AND DISEASES

WHENEVER you are hoeing or weeding between bushes, check that the pests and diseases detailed here are not becoming established. When treated early, few of them are a radical problem. But if left, bushes may become so damaged that they are best dug up and burned immediately.

Viruses are sometimes a problem and these are usually transmitted by sucking pests, such as aphids (greenfly). The virus usually reveals itself as pale areas, often irregular but occasionally in a fancy pattern. Although viruses seldom kill plants, they are an eyesore and diminish a plant's vigour. Never use virus-infected plants as propagation material.

Balling disfigures rose buds; the petals fail to open and subsequently turn brown. Excessive and continuous rain causes it, especially to roses with large, thin petals. It is not a disease. Nevertheless, it is a disfiguring disorder.

APHIDS *(greenfly) cluster on soft shoots and around and slightly below flower buds. They suck sap, distort growth and transmit viruses. Spray with a systemic insecticide as soon as they are seen.*

BLACK SPOT *is a fungal disease that causes black spots on leaves. Spray with a fungicide several times. Remove and burn fallen, infected leaves to prevent the infection spreading.*

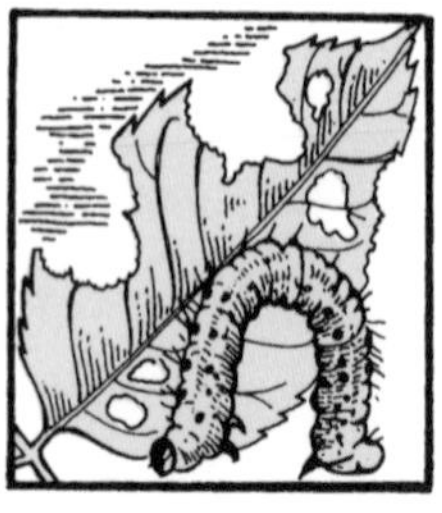

CATERPILLARS *frequently chew leaves, creating irregularly-shaped holes, especially in young leaves. Pick off and destroy the caterpillars and regularly spray with an insecticide.*

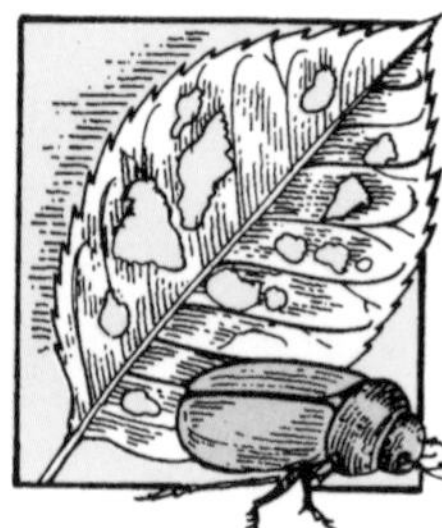

COCKCHAFER BEETLES *(May Bug and reddish-brown) chew irregular-shaped holes in leaves in early and mid-summer. Pick off and destroy the beetles and spray with an insecticide.*

COCKCHAFER BEETLES *such as those of the Garden and Rose Chafer types chew flower buds, causing severe damage to them. Pick off and destroy the beetles and use an insecticide immediately.*

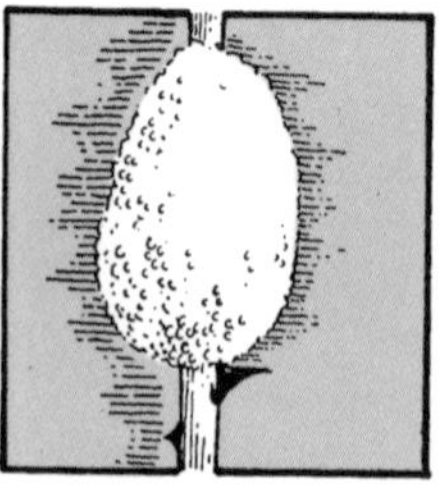

CUCKOO-SPIT, *a white and frothy spittle enclosing Froghoppers, is an eyesore. Leaves may wilt and be distorted. Spray with water to dislodge, remove by hand or use an insecticide.*

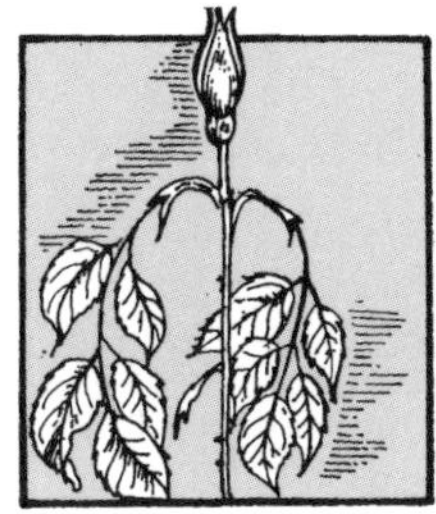

DIE-BACK, *a disease that causes tips of shoots progressively to die downwards, has several causes: frost, canker, waterlogging and diseases. Cut out and burn infected parts.*

LEAF-ROLLING SAWFLY *causes leaves to roll, enclosing a greyish-green grub. Leaves later shrivel and die. Pick off and burn small infestations, or prevent damage with an insecticide.*

LEAFHOPPERS *create pale, mottled areas on leaves. Growth is checked, leaves become distorted and may fall off if the attack is severe. Spray with a systemic insecticide.*

MILDEW *is a common disease, covering leaves, stems and buds with a white powder. If neglected, plants eventually die. Spray plants regularly and keep soil moist.*

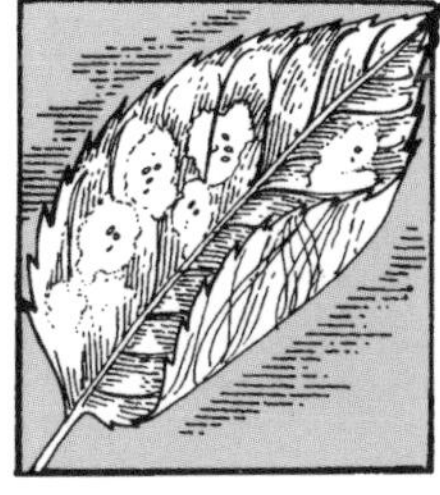

RED SPIDER MITES *cause bronzed patches on upper surfaces of leaves and fine webbing on the undersides. Mist-spray plants with clean water and use an insecticide.*

ROSE SLUGWORM *creates skeletonized leaves by eating soft parts between veins. Greenish-yellow grubs can often be seen on the surface. Spray with an insecticide.*

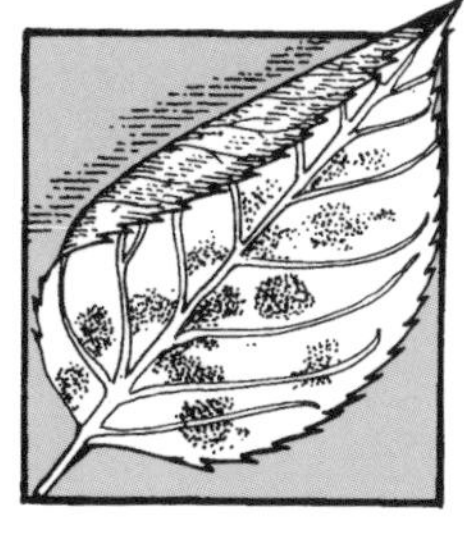

RUST *is not common, but difficult to eradicate. Orange swellings appear on the undersides of leaves. Spray plants regularly especially if it is a widespread problem in your area.*

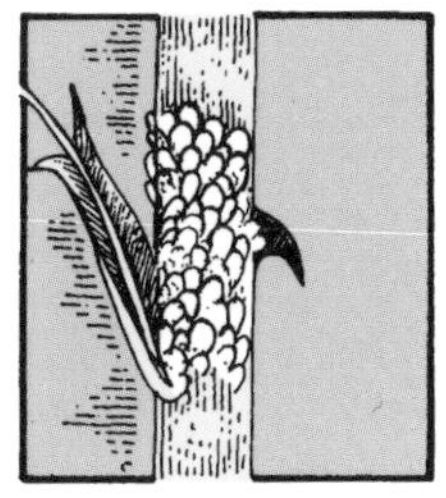

ROSE SCALE *is most often seen on old and neglected bushes. Scurfy scales cluster on stems. Wipe off colonies with methylated spirits (rubbing alcohol) and use a systemic insecticide.*

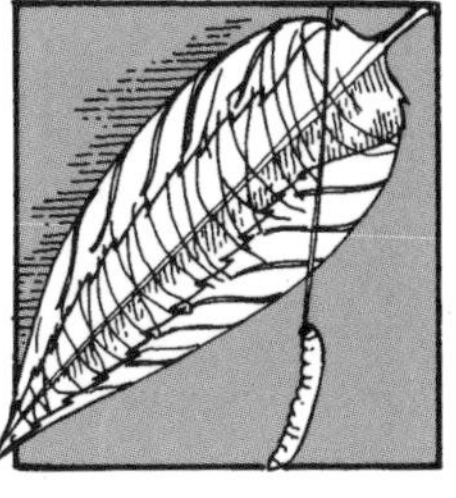

TORTRIX MOTHS *chew irregular holes in leaves, then spin fine threads to hold the edges together. Pick off and destroy the larvae if the infestation is light, or spray with an insecticide.*

ROSE CALENDAR

SPRING

In early spring, check all pruning tools. Gloves and kneelers are also essential, together with strong loppers if there are old roses with thick stems at their base to be pruned. If you are left-handed, remember that there are special secateurs to suit you; they make pruning a much easier job.

In cold areas, do not begin pruning too early, as it might encourage the development of young shoots that will be damaged by late spring frosts.

- Ensure all pruning tools are sharp; if blunt they cause stems to be damaged (14–15).
- Plant container-grown roses at any time when the soil is not frozen or waterlogged (12–13).
- In early spring, prune roses that were planted in autumn or during winter (14–15).
- Bushes planted in spring are pruned immediately after planting (14–15).
- If late spring is dry, water the soil around roses, especially if they were planted during the previous winter and are not yet fully established (16–17).
- In warm springs and if weeds are starting to grow it is possible to apply weed-killing chemicals from a watering-can fitted with a dribble-bar. Never do this during strong winds (16–17).
- Mulch roses in late spring or early summer. But first make sure you hoe off weeds and apply a feed (16–17).
- In early spring, re-firm soil around rose bushes to ensure it is in contact with roots (16–17).
- Check all ties on standard roses to ensure they are firm but not constrictive (16–17).
- Start feeding roses in late spring (18–19).

SUMMER

This is a season of great activity when growing roses.

- Regularly check bush roses to see if sucker shoots are growing from ground-level. Remove them (16–17).
- Suckers sometimes grow from the stems of standard roses. Regularly cut them off (16–17).
- Water the soil around roses if it becomes dry (16–17).
- Remove dead flowers from bush roses (16–17).
- Do not remove dead flowers from Shrub Roses grown for their heps (fruits) (16–17).
- Apply weed-killing chemicals from a watering-can fitted with a dribble-bar. However, never do this when strong winds are blowing (16–17).
- Disbud Hybrid Tea blooms that are being grown to be exhibited at shows (16–17).
- Mulch roses in late spring or early summer. But first hoe off weeds and apply a feed (16–17).
- When cutting roses from bushes for home decoration, use a sharp knife or secateurs and do not take them all from the same position on the plant (16–17).
- Plant container-grown roses at any time when the soil is workable (12–13).
- Start feeding roses in late spring, then continue with further feeds in summer (18).
- Apply a foliar feed to exhibition roses (18).
- When growing roses for exhibition, prepare the blooms by tying soft string or wool around half-open buds (19).
- Place cone-shaped bloom-protectors over exhibition roses to prevent rain spoiling them (19).
- Support weak stems on exhibition roses by wiring them (19).

AUTUMN

Some roses continue flowering into mid and late-autumn, but most have finished by late summer. When leaves fall off plants in autumn, clear them up and burn them, especially if infected with diseases or pests. If left, they help to continue the problem into the following season.

- Plant container-grown roses at any time when the soil is workable (12–13).
- Plant bare-rooted roses from late autumn to late winter, whenever the soil is not frozen or waterlogged (12–13).
- Plant bare-rooted roses as soon as they are received. If there is to be a long delay, bury their roots in a trench (12–13).
- Before planting bare-rooted roses, prepare them by trimming back their shoots and roots (12–13).
- Before planting bare-rooted roses, always check that the roots are plump and moist. If necessary, place them in a bucket of water (12–13).
- Transplant established roses while they are in their dormant period, from late autumn to late winter (12–13).
- When planting a climber, do not position the roots directly next to a wall, as the soil may be too dry (12–13).
- When planting a standard rose, first knock in the stake (12–13).
- In late autumn or early winter, cut back long stems to reduce the amount of foliage. This helps to prevent the roots of plants being rocked in the soil when buffeted by strong winds during winter (14–15).
- Check all ties on standard roses to ensure they are firm but not constrictive (16–17). It is essential they are secure, in preparation for strong winter winds.

WINTER

This is the season of preparing soil for the following year.

- Check areas where roses are to be planted to ensure the drainage is good (10–11).
- Plan new rose beds and assess if the soil is heavy or light. Improve them (10–11).
- Check the acidity or alkalinity of soil where new rose beds are planned. Roses grow best in a pH of 6.0 to 6.5.
- If soil is extremely chalky, consider forming raised beds in which to grow roses (10–11).
- If excessively chalky soil cannot be improved, grow lime-tolerant roses (10–11).
- Single dig soil (10–11).
- Double dig soil being converted from pasture land (10–11).
- When planning new rose beds, check that the position is suitable (10–11)
- If branches of trees need to be removed to allow more light and air to reach plants – as well as to prevent rain dripping off them – winter is the time to tackle this work (10–11).
- Plant container-grown roses at any time when the soil is workable (12–13).
- Plant bare-rooted roses from late autumn to late winter, whenever the soil is not frozen or waterlogged (12–13).
- Plant bare-rooted roses as soon as possible. If there is a long delay, bury their roots in a trench (12–13).
- Before planting bare-rooted roses, trim their shoots and roots (12–13).
- Before planting bare-rooted roses, always check that the roots are moist (12–13).
- Transplant established roses when dormant (12–13).
- When planting a climber, do not position near a wall (12–13).

GLOSSARY OF ROSE TERMS

ACID SOIL: *Soil which has a pH of less than 7.0.*

AMERICAN ROSE SOCIETY: *A North American rose society founded in 1899.*

ANTHER: *The part of a flower which produces pollen. In some roses the anthers are golden and attractive.*

AXIL: *Correctly, the angle between a leaf stalk and the shoot which bears it. More usually, it is the junction of a leaf or shoot with a stem.*

BALLING: *A physiological disorder, when the outside petals of a flower cling together (see page 58).*

BARE-ROOTED: *Young rose plants are often sold with bare roots; they have been dug up during their dormant period to be sent to a customer for replanting.*

BLEEDING: *The loss of sap from a stem as a result of being pruned too late in spring, or early summer, after sap has started to rise.*

BLIND SHOOT: *A physiological disorder that occurs when a shoot fails to develop a flowerbud. These shoots should be completely cut out.*

BLOOM: *An alternative term for a flower or group of flowers. It can also mean a waxy, powdery coating.*

BLOWN: *When a flower is fully open and the petals are starting to fade or fall off.*

BRACT: *A small leaf-like growth on a flower stalk.*

BUD*: A flower before it opens. Inside a bud, petals and other flower parts are protected by overlapping, scale-like growths.*

BUD UNION: *The position where a plant is budded.*

BUDDING: *A method of propagation, when a bud of the varietal part is united with a root-stock of known vigour and quality.*

BUTTON EYE: *Occurs at the centre of flowers on some Old Roses. A few petals fold inwards to form a button.*

CALYX: *Green, somewhat scale-like tissue which protects a flower when at its bud stage.*

COMPOST: *This has two meanings. One is vegetable material placed in a heap and encouraged to decompose so that eventually it can be dug into soil or used to form a mulch. The other meaning is a compost (mixture of sharp sand, moist peat and sterilized soil) in which seeds are sown, cuttings rooted and plants grown.*

CULTIVAR: *A variety raised in cultivation. Properly, the vast majority of modern rose varieties should be known as cultivars, but as the term variety is by far the better known this has been used throughout this book. Also, variety is a far more friendly term than cultivar.*

CUTTING: *A healthy piece of plant, detached and encouraged to form roots.*

DEAD-HEADING: *The removal of faded or dead flowers to encourage the development of more blooms.*

DE-SHOOTING: *The removal of shoots to ensure that the remaining ones have more light and air.*

DIE-BACK: *When a shoot decays down from its tip.*

DISBUDDING: *The removal of small buds from around a main flower to encourage its development.*

DOUBLE-FLOWERED: *Refers to the number of petals in a flower. Some double flowers are said to be 'moderately full' (21 to 29 petals), others 'full' (30 to 39 petals), while some are 'very full' (40 or more petals).*

FLORIBUNDA ROSES: *These are now properly called Cluster-flowered Bush Roses. However, they are invariably listed in catalogues by their earlier name, which is better known to gardeners.*

FLUSH: *A period when flowers are opening. Some varieties have repeated flushes of flowers during summer.*

FOLIAR FEEDING: *Spraying foliage with fertilizers to apply plant foods.*

FUNGICIDE: *A chemical used to prevent or control the presence of disease.*

GENUS: *A botanical classification of related plants. Within a genus there could be one or more species.*

GRANDIFLORA: *A North American term for large Floribundas with Hybrid Tea-like flowers.*

HEELING-IN: *The temporary planting of bare-rooted plants in winter, while waiting for the weather to improve so that they can be planted in beds and borders.*

HEP: *The fruit of a rose. Also known as a hip.*

HIP: *An alternative name for hep.*

HYBRID: *An offspring from two unrelated parents.*

HYBRID TEA: *These roses are now properly known as Large-flowered Bush Roses. However, they are invariably listed in catalogues by their earlier name, by which they are better known to gardeners. Therefore, throughout this book the earlier name is used.*

MAIDEN: *A plant in its first year after being budded or grafted.*

MULCH: *The formation of a layer of organic material around plants – but not touching their stems.*

MUTATION: *The spontaneous change in a part of a plant. This includes greater or lesser vigour, large or small flowers, and a change in colour. This often leads to the creation of new varieties. They are also known as sports.*

NEUTRAL: *Refers to soil which is neither acid nor alkaline, having a pH of about 7.0.*

ONCE-FLOWERING: *A single flush of flowers, generally lasting for several weeks. Some varieties with this nature also produce a few flowers in autumn, but not sufficiently to be called a second flush.*

PEDICEL: *A flower stalk.*

pH: *A scale from 0 to 14 that defines the alkalinity or acidity of soil. A pH of 7.0 is neutral: figures above this indicate increasing alkalinity, and below show more acidity.*

POLLINATION: *The transference of pollen from anther (male part of a flower) to stigma (female part). Fertilization does not necessarily follow pollination.*

PROPAGATION: *Creating further plants. In the case of roses, this is usually by budding, although some can be layered, raised from cuttings or from seeds.*

QUARTERED: *Refers to the arrangement of petals in a flower, when it appears to be formed of four distinctive parts. Many of the Old Roses (Old Fashioned Roses) have this attractive feature.*

RECURRENT: *The production of two or more flushes of flowers during the same flowering season.*

REMONTANT: *Means the same as recurrent.*

REPEAT FLOWERING: *Means the same as recurrent.*

ROOT-STOCK: *The root part of a rose bush. Varieties are budded on to it.*

ROSA: *The genus to which all roses belong.*

SCION: *The term for the bud which is budded on to the root-stock.*

SEMI-DOUBLE FLOWERS: *Refers to the number of petals present (8 to 20) in a rose.*

SINGLE FLOWERS: *Refers to the number of petals present (less than 8).*

SPORT: *A popular and widely-used term for a mutation.*

STIPULE: *A leaf-like growth which arises at the base of a leaf stalk.*

SUCKER: *Growth which arises from the root-stock of bush roses, or stems of standard-type roses. Suckers must be removed.*

SYSTEMIC INSECTICIDE: *A pesticide which makes a plant's sap-stream toxic to insects.*

TAKE: *a term that indicates the successful uniting of a bud with a root-stock.*

TRUSS: *A flower cluster.*

VARIETY: *At one time, all variations within a species were known as varieties. Now, correctly, varieties raised in cultivation are known as cultivars. However, the term variety is much better known than cultivar (which to many people is an unfriendly term).*

INDEX